Happy Decorating,

Love

Adri

EVERY
THING

ABIGAIL AHERN

EVERY THING

A MAXIMALIST STYLE GUIDE

PAVILION

WHAT IS
MAXIMALISM?

Full disclosure:
I am an unabashed maximalist.

One of the reasons I am so obsessed with maximalist interiors is that they stir up emotions, offering a much-needed respite from minimalism and mid-century quietness. Maximalism is the most explorative of styles, nothing is off limits. Through experimentation with materiality, colour, form, vintage finds and modern pieces it's an aesthetic that pulls in and weaves together different periods and styles that are distinctive, expressive narratives. It's a highly stylized type of decor and it holds comfort as its very centre. It's a full-on sensory experience that lifts your spirits and provides inspiration in a way that minimalism just can't.

I think maximalist interiors have had a bad rap in the past because spaces can look like they've been decorated by someone who's had seven cups of coffee while nursing a hangover: chaotic and messy with an overwhelming thoughtlessness and disarray that feels jarring and not at all serene. Yet it doesn't have to feel that way. I'm championing a new kind of maximalism, one that – when you get it right – feels considered, curated and magical.

There is such an emotional quality to maximalist interiors because they require you to draw upon things you love. I'll be unravelling my ideas for creating a sensory-stimulating home, where a visual cacophony of pieces tie in together, harmonize and intrigue, and also contrast and excite. In so doing we'll be mixing fancy with friendly, gritty with glam, feminine with masculine, dainty with weighty and, above all, we'll create a home you'll never want to leave.

Here's how...

DEVELOPING A SENSE OF STYLE

I am a huge believer that by adding considered colours, textures, patterns and accents you'll create spaces that solicit conversation and evoke immense personal pleasure.

Maximalist interiors cram in a wealth of experiences in every space, mixing edgy pieces with vintage treasures, and refined items with raw, unique, one-off finds. It's one of the most interesting and individual design styles out there. It pushes boundaries and challenges rules and in so doing provokes an emotional response.

Nothing is off limits! Having said that, I'm not talking about neon pink walls, with plastic pigeons and a large dollop of leopard print thrown in. If you love that vibe, go for it, it's just not for me. I am talking about partnering high end with low end, high street with handcrafted, vintage with modern. My kind of interior is decorating with intention rather than just frivolously plonking stuff everywhere. I am a believer that by adding considered colours, textures, patterns and accents you'll create spaces that solicit conversation and evoke immense personal pleasure.

Whether your place is big or small, owned or rented, whether you live uptown or downtown, on the coast or in the country, maximalist interiors are all about surrounding yourself with things that you love that make you (and your home) feel a little bit cooler, a little bit more glamorous, and that resonate with the heart.

Whatever style your home is, it should feel like a place free from rules and authority where you can do whatever you like. I know that when I get home and put the key in the lock I enter a space that calms me, inspires me and makes me feel a whole lot happier. I've escaped into my own universe and my home is a reflection of my interior self! If all of that sounds too profound, fear not, we are going to deep dive into how to create a home that reflects you, by balancing colours, patterns, rich fabrics, textures and eclectic furnishings, all in one room.

ASK QUESTIONS

I know first hand from the classes I teach all over the globe, as well as hold in my own pad every month, that many people struggle with finding their own sense of style. This might sound a tad gung-ho but it's actually easier than you may think. It just takes a pair of fresh eyes and about a zillion questions. Start with taking a walk through your home and ask yourself the following:

→ What stands out, what catches your eye?
→ How do you feel in the space?
→ Are your walls too plain?
→ Do you like the paint colour?
→ What pieces do you love?
→ What colours do you like?
→ What styles are you drawn to?
→ Do you have any hobbies, activities or collections that need to be factored in?

We live in the world of apps; there are apps for everything, and there are some great ones out there to help you with creating floor plans – you simply hold your phone up to the wall and watch it scan the circumference of the room. There are other apps that give you the ability to place 3D models of real furniture in your own room. Not sure what that brass pendant will look like over your island? You don't have to guess anymore. Cool, hey? See my Little Black Book on page 244 for more details.

EMOTIVE DESIGN

I always design each and every space in my own house around a mood or emotion, and I ask myself continually how I want to feel in each room. My answer is usually a complex one as fundamentally I want to feel relaxed but I also want to feel tantalized and bedazzled. I want to feel cocooned and wrapped up in the squishiest of blankets.

Believe it or not, your decorating choices totally affect your emotions and how you feel in a space. The colour on your walls can make you feel relaxed, or – if you get it wrong – anxious. Your decor can have a profound effect on how you feel too. The lighting you select and the interiors you choose all contribute to making you feel happy, relaxed and more engaged, as long as you buy from the heart and don't follow trends.

Ask yourself how you want to feel in your space. For example, because I want to feel cocooned, I'll work backwards and write down what style of furnishings does that for me, from deeply slouchy chairs to inky and soft colours which help me feel protected.

Lose the fear! I hear about this so very often in my classes – the fear of making mistakes. It's so easy to get hung up on the fear of getting it wrong that we do nothing at all and that beige paint on the wall stays up there forever. Maximalist interiors can feel daunting, so it's super easy to sit on the fence. Yet when you decorate differently and break boundaries it becomes addictive. You can create magical spaces. My biggest piece of advice – and this relates to overcoming a fear of anything (including spiders) – is to slowly build up your confidence! Start small. Rather than looking at your whole room and panicking about maximalizing the whole thing, zone it into small sections. It's almost impossible to figure out everything all in one go but when you break rooms down into zones it's so much easier. Once you get started, you will have the confidence to move on.

As I have just said, it's easy to play it safe when it comes to decorating, but the trouble with playing it safe is that it doesn't allow you to inject personality into your home. When you add a bold print or colour, it quickly and easily transforms the space. I always rely on my gut feeling when it comes to decision-making risks.

By simply juxtaposing materials, painting a wall in a tantalizing hue, changing the layout, adding pattern and texture, or overdosing on lighting, you can change how someone feels in a space.

20

Recognize those feelings of discomfort and if you find you have to talk yourself into something (like a colour or an item of furniture), then that particular hue or piece just might not be right for you. Conversely though, you need an open mind to think outside of the box. Unexpected choices give a space spirit and an edge. If you choose statement pieces, remember to ground your space with quieter, more restrained details, as too many starlets in one room will create too much drama.

Avoid themes if you can. The trouble with theming (and it's a very easy thing to do) is that your space will look like it's just popped out of the pages of a catalogue and therefore won't read as a true reflection of who you are. I think one of the reasons maximalism has taken the interior and fashion world by storm lately is that people are gaining a new sense of confidence in their own voices. Whether that is a reaction to the political climate, or down to certain films and television shows illustrating some truly beautiful maximalist spaces, who knows, but there is more individuality, warmth and personality in interiors than ever before. Theming will restrict you far too much, so – in my humble opinion – avoid it. Think of yourself like a poet or writer, they are artists who draw people into the world they have created. We are going to be doing the very same thing with interiors.

I get the biggest adrenaline rush when people enter my space and their jaws hit the floor. They sigh and gasp and smile – they don't know where to look. Their eyes are drawn in so many different directions, so they feel excited, engaged and tantalized all at once. It's so energizing to think that you can lift someone's spirits in this way, both your own and your guests! By simply juxtaposing materials, painting a wall in a tantalizing hue, changing the layout, adding pattern and texture, or overdosing on lighting, you can change how someone feels in a space.

THINK OF YOURSELF LIKE
A POET OR WRITER, THEY
ARE ARTISTS WHO DRAW
PEOPLE INTO THE WORLD
THEY HAVE CREATED.

As we progress through the book you will notice common elements in many of the interiors shown in the images. They are generally harmonious, they tend to balance, the colour palette is often restrained (four or five hues at most) and there is a lot of friction going on. All of which we will discuss in more detail later on.

Believe it or not, living with maximalist interiors has got nothing to do with being materialistic. Instead it's about having pieces in your life that remind you of something: a trip to Asia; a memory of a loved one; something your kids painted. It's about curating memories, and you can't do that if you live in a white box where everything is behind a push drawer with no handles! No stuff, no intrigue. No intrigue, no magic – simple as that!

Layering is a key component. The more layers you have in a room the more tantalizing it is for the eye, because it doesn't quite know where to land. As we progress through the book I will be showing you how to layer and style up your space. You'll become more confident (as I did). I went from pale walls to dark walls, fireplaces with nothing on them to fireplaces with lots on them. Bare floors to floors layered with the most intoxicating collection of rugs. Some things I found on the high street, others are from flea markets. Some I stumbled across in souks in Morocco and the odd one I got from galleries. Magic started to happen as I began to add more and more things. I grew more confident, I felt more inspired. I looked outwards more, across cultures, styles, ages and eras and it's made my interiors so much more alluring.

Look at curated images online now and everyone seems to be getting excited about incredibly opulent, complicated and intriguing ways of decorating, which is so empowering.

WHERE TO START?

We live in exciting times when it comes to interiors. We can buy from any corner of the globe and design is suddenly getting very clever and very complex.

In the past, most people decorating their homes opted for the simplistic, combining neutrals and accenting with natural materials, almost looking at homes more as a commodity. Look at curated images online now and everyone seems to be getting very excited about incredibly opulent, complicated and intriguing ways of decorating, which is so empowering.

There are a few key aesthetics out there that it's worth being aware of, as it's pretty crucial to identify the core aspects of each one in order to develop your own sense of style. In reality you'll probably want to blend different elements from various styles rather than sticking to just one as the most exciting interiors these days take inspiration from so many different vibes.

→ Let's start with my least favourite style, **Scandinavian**! Blonde walls with white wood, anyone? I am being a trifle mean, it's actually a combo of beauty, simplicity and (the bit I am not so keen on) functionality. White walls reign supreme and it's a neutral-heavy palette; streamlined and ultra clean. Playful accent colours are peppered in but in general it's very understated. It's taken the world by storm because it's an easy way to decorate. You don't have to think too much and with a focus on simplicity and minimalism it doesn't take too much work to create this most unfussy of looks.

→ **Traditional** interiors are timeless and take their cue from the 18th and 19th centuries. Often lambasted for being boring and staid, this style consistently creates calm, orderly spaces. Symmetry is big, woods are often dark, and rich colours and elaborate and ornate details, as well as luxe fabrics like velvet and silk, abound. It's a very structural style which is why I like it best when used in combination with more modern styles.

→ **Industrial style** champions exposed steel, distressed wooden elements, copper accents and exposed bulbs. It's a rustic, warm warehouse look. It's a style that celebrates manufacturing and mechanical ingenuity with an appreciation of raw unfinished surfaces like timber trusses and concrete.

→ **Mid-century modern** is characterized by organic shapes, minimalist silhouettes and refined lines. It's a highly desired style and relevant materials include moulded plastic, plywood and aluminium. It's fuss free and I'm constantly dipping into this style.

→ **French provincial** is a warm style, colours are often earthy, woods abound and there is an overarching farmhouse vibe. Natural inspiration is abundant, as are soft linens and lots of texture.

→ **Boho style** reflects a carefree vibe with few rules. Think globally inspired pieces along with vintage finds. It's an eclectic, warm, super-cosy style. I love it as there is a laissez-faire attitude that goes along with it – the perfect match for maximalist interiors.

→ **Eclectic** interiors incorporate elements from various cultures and all of the styles mentioned above. It's the hardest one to pull off and, as with maximalist interiors, it's the thoughtful editing and the linking of disparate elements through texture, material, style and colour that make it work.

Something to remember (and don't get too cross with me when I tell you this): your home will never be totally finished. Even when you've dipped into some (or all) of the styles above and decorated the whole place, a few years down the line you'll pick something up, pop it on the wall or floor and it will make you want to change everything! Not throw things away, just rearrange and move stuff around. That's the fun part, and anyway, nature is never finished so why should our surroundings be? Your home will be in an ever-changing flux of addition and subtraction. That is what I love about maximalist interiors, they are never locked into one single style, they look and feel constantly switched up and they are always evolving.

This is such an eclectic and varied way of decorating, as we are pulling from many different styles. It's really important to look at your space as a whole, so as you transition from room to room it flows and feels consistent. I believe that if you go maximalist, you should go maximalist throughout, so everything gets an upgrade, which is reflected through the entire space.

Remember to introduce some kind of imperfection here and there. Sounds odd I know, but it's an important element and is often neglected. Maximalism is not about filling homes with the latest on trend chairs, sofas or lamps, instead think about maybe introducing an old frayed rug, or a basket that's a little bit worn. Pieces that feel authentic rather than everything feeling impeccably finished. If there are any particular features of the building like old worn floorboards, or a fireplace, allow them to take centre stage. This all adds individuality and character. Also, I always try to introduce a few handmade things into my interiors. One-of-a-kind objects, from plates to vases to tables, that have unique characteristics and that almost appear to tell the story of their makers. They are not perfectly formed – it's a return to the artisanal and the handcrafted. Fingerprints of process and technique, pieces that aren't perfectly polished or manicured – these add so much into a space, making it feel more layered, and artier somehow, more unpredictable and unique.

It's really important to look at your space as a whole, so as you transition from room to room it flows and feels consistent.

IF YOU CHOOSE STATEMENT
PIECES, REMEMBER TO
GROUND YOUR SPACE WITH
QUIETER, MORE RESTRAINED
DETAILS, AS TOO MANY
STARLETS IN ONE ROOM WILL
CREATE TOO MUCH DRAMA.

This new wave of maximalism is far cleverer and more intriguing than just filling homes with a hodge-podge of stuff. It's not a pastiche of the past where random assortments of things fill shelves and look and feel cluttered. There is order within. Express your own style – whether that has a tribal influence, or is maybe more glam, tropical, Parisian or rustic even – it matters not. What matters is that you love it.

One final point: you are going to make the odd mistake along the way. Decorating in this fashion is one of the hardest things to do and I make mistakes all the time. However, from all these mistakes I have learned something in the process which has led me to making better (and cooler) decisions. I've painted walls the wrong colour. Once I even got Graham, my husband, to wood clad all the exterior walls in our garden in a horizontal fashion, only at the end of the day to take them all down – they looked so bad! I only appreciated after he had done all the work that verticals made the garden grander and horizontals way too short. I learnt this the hard way, but now I have the most beautiful, magical garden on the planet!

I'm here to help and guide you so you don't have to worry too much about making mistakes. We are going to design spaces together that not only look amazing but will also be a reflection of your own personality and style. Maximalist interiors don't happen by chance, they are carefully planned and curated. With all my insider knowledge you'll soon be thinking creatively and outside of the box and designing spaces that are stimulating and sensory, multi-faceted and layered. I'm so excited!

Maximalist interiors don't happen by chance, they are carefully planned and curated.

EXPRESSING YOURSELF

Just because you add in more objects, more patterns, more textures and more stuff doesn't mean good design has to be compromised.

The best maximalist interiors have a strong identity with a clear sense of what they are. Get it wrong, however, and they can read as chaotic and messy. They will send you running for the hills and the pills simultaneously! There is nowhere to hide with maximalist interiors – it's an aesthetic that embraces pattern, colour, texture and all-out 'stuff'. I know that this can feel a little overwhelming for anyone who has not dabbled in it before, but don't panic. As much as I love the irreverence of tossing rules aside, there are certain guidelines for maximalist style that make the task of decorating in this fashion foolproof.

This book embraces a new kind of maximalism, one in which flamboyant creativity is front and centre. Out-there patterns, sweet-shop colours and cartoon shapes are on the back burner. I'm going to show you how you can combine many opposing, complicated elements and be playful, but always in a beautiful, sophisticated and restrained fashion. Just because you add in more objects, more patterns, more textures and more stuff, doesn't mean good design has to be compromised.

Maximalist interiors have had a bit of a bad rap in the past as many people think of them as messy. They don't have to be. This way of decorating isn't easy, we are not decorating by numbers here, but you do have to have a few rules up your sleeve to make it all work. It may feel uncomfortable at first, as you'll be putting yourself and your home in what might be an entirely new and unfamiliar situation. Friends, family and colleagues might try to put you off, but

from all my years in the business, I would like to say at this point that when you feel uncomfortable, ultimately you are doing something right.

You're dipping your toe outside of your safe space and the greatest risk is not taking any risk at all. Listen to no one – other than me of course! With a good set of guidelines and some great curation we are going to design a home you will never want to leave, that is personal and unique to you. Think of it like this: we are going on the most fabulous journey together and in so doing we'll create spaces that tantalize, intrigue and excite. I love this comment from Oprah Winfrey: 'When you are pioneering anything or introducing new ideas to a culture, you get criticized.' Remain open-minded, embrace these very loose guidelines and you will not fail. I promise!

THE BARE BONES
When people ask me where they should start, I always suggest that they first consider the walls and the floors.

Let's begin with the walls, one of the biggest and most impactful ways of expressing yourself in a room. A beautiful wall treatment is sure to enchant, whether you opt for fabric, paper, paint, cement, tile or wood – the world is your oyster. The walls are generally the largest surfaces in a room so make sure that you put them front and centre when it comes to figuring out the colour and treatment. Make it as

40

effortless and as chic as you possibly can. Getting the walls right will take your home from just ok to really great. Think of the walls as your solid base that lays down the foundations.

Treatments are numerous but one of the most popular is paint. Figuring out your paint colour early on is a good place to start. We will be discussing colour in more detail later on, but contrary to popular belief you don't have to have a dark palette to create a layered sumptuous home. Anything goes! Paint finish is very important, just

as important as the colour in fact, and can have a major effect on the character of your room and the atmosphere you want to create. The majority of finishes are water based, which is great as water based paints don't require a pre-treatment and can be used on almost every surface. Sheen options vary according to the manufacturer but I always plump for matt, which is the least reflective of the lot. It's a good choice for maximalist interiors, as you don't want the wall finish to compete too much with what's going on the wall.

THINK OF IT LIKE THIS:
WE ARE GOING ON THE
MOST FABULOUS JOURNEY
TOGETHER AND IN SO
DOING WE'LL CREATE
SPACES THAT TANTALIZE,
INTRIGUE AND EXCITE.

That gallery wall will look far cooler if it's not competing with the background too much. Matt walls read as super luxurious. If you have sheen, it tends to distract the eye a tad, as the light reflects off it. But there are lots of options out there.

→ Eggshell and satin paints have some reflectivity and are often used in demanding environments like bathrooms and kitchens. Gloss paint is obviously the most reflective and it is the most durable and can stand multiple cleanings. It's usually used on baseboards, mouldings and doors but can also be applied to walls and ceilings, giving them instant luminosity.

→ There is a big comeback right now for lime plaster and tadelakt (a waterproof lime plaster often used in Moroccan interiors, but now installed in more and more residences the world over). When applied to walls it almost makes you feel like you're a living within a Rothko painting. This resurgence is thanks to plaster-loving influential designers such as Axel Vervoordt and Vincent Van Duysen.

→ There's no denying that wallpaper is a big commitment and scares many people. From delicate floral tapestries to bold graphic patterns it certainly provides plenty of visual interest. Don't feel you have to go all out crazy with pattern on your walls; I certainly don't. There are so many beautiful papers out there that emulate concrete, wood or tile and have the most incredible texture.

→ Wood is another beautiful treatment for walls. Simple, soothing and warm, it's impossible to resist and has such welcoming qualities.

→ Brick – rough and bare, or painted out – adds a beautiful timeless texture to any interior, not forgetting warmth and character. And let's not overlook tiles – from cement tiles to irridescent pearlized ones, to geometric and even floral, the possibilities are endless.

Ensure that you take time to consider what is going on your walls. It will set the mood and atmosphere in each and every space.

Though the flooring may not be the first thing to garner our attention when we walk into a home, it is crucial for a cohesive, enviable interior. No matter how much attention you pay to your decor it may never look exactly right if the bones of the room aren't thoughtfully designed. From warm and homely wood to industrial concrete, from laminate to rugs and carpets, your choice of flooring will have a big impact on your interior. Oh, and if you don't love your current floor, panic not, as a great rug will always help you hide ugly flooring!

Floors are so important. It doesn't matter if you have hardwood floors, area rugs, wall-to-wall carpeting, or stone, your flooring will dictate to a large degree how you layer your space. There are two schools of thought when it comes to flooring: either stay neutral without much colour or pattern, or go colourful and patterned. You will have more options if you stay neutral when it comes to furnishings, finishing touches, accent colours and upholstery. Or, totally ignore that and go for the more patterned and colourful option and draw upon those hues and reflect them into your furnishings. There is no wrong and no right. The most important thing is to have a plan, otherwise you will end up with a chaotic circus effect, with far too many things going on.

Maximalist interiors need harmony and balance otherwise they read like a hot mess.

Ceilings are so often forgotten, yet they are integral to creating a beautiful looking maximalist home. All great designers remember to look up, it's a place to create design magic, and has a huge impact on the surrounding areas. Suspend a pendant or chandelier from the ceiling and you create subtle light effects. One of my favourite ways of sprucing up a space is painting the ceilings out the same colour as your walls. We're pushing boundaries here, as I know this scares a lot of people, but I happen to think it's one of the most important things you can do to a space. Be it big, small, old and wonky, new and modern, pokey or palatial, this simple trick will immediately make the space feel grander, without fail. When you paint the ceiling out, lines become blurred, so you can't quite tell where the walls end and the ceiling begins. The space feels more sophisticated somehow as well as bigger, so it's a super cool trick for small spaces and spaces with low ceilings. Everything is now camouflaged (door and window frames and skirtings should also be painted out the same hue) and the eye is forced to concentrate on the pieces in the room. They now feel grander, cooler and edgier!

RULES FOR SUCCESS

Now we've dealt with the bones of the room let's talk about a few further guidelines. Maximalist interiors need harmony and balance otherwise they read like a hot mess. If you search 'maximalist interiors' online, up will come a riot of extravagant, over-the-top spaces. I'm talking exuberantly papered rooms, knick-knacks everywhere, brightly coloured walls, with not one bare surface. This is great if you happen to love that vibe, but I'm championing a new kind of maximalism. One that is slightly more restrained, tangible even, and perhaps a little spiritual. Of course there is visual cacophony, but this kind of maximalism is unimpeachably chic versus chaotic, hence the importance of harmony and balance.

Whether your room embraces maximalism or not (it's even more important if it does) the whole space needs to read as visually grounding as possible. Tie in colours, shapes and textures. Don't go all matchy-matchy on me, as that just reads like a big yawn and is really quite dull. Just make sure there is some sort of connection and cohesion. I unify rooms through rugs, plants, colour, materials and lighting. Although everything is different, it all feels very interconnected.

Ensure that you take time to consider what is going on your walls. It will set the mood and atmosphere in each and every space.

I'm about to confuse you even further, because as much as we want things to feel harmonious, we also need to introduce an element of friction. Friction is fundamental in interior design and even more so with these more-on-more spaces. If everything were one note – let's say, for example, glossy walls with shiny floors, leather furniture, glass coffee table – do you see how one-dimensional and flat that would feel? In order to keep things interesting we need to place as many different textures and tactile elements and materials together in a room as possible. That might be an old woolly rug on a smooth polished concrete floor, or slubby handwoven cushions on a leather sofa. Or handthrown ceramics on a wooden coffee table. What you are doing is becoming a mixologist.

You're blending silks with wools, leathers with grainy woods, glass with ceramics. All these elements contrast yet complement, and give you a beautiful finished look.

You can also create friction by mixing styles. A modern lamp on an old vintage table for example, or a new chair reupholstered in a vintage-style fabric. Pair the old with the new, the fancy with the friendly, the raw with the refined, the grit with the glam – then the magic happens!

Something I teach in my classes is that making a home feel beautiful is not down to some huge expensive artwork or grand chandelier but the feelings that you evoke. For example, you can create the most incredible feeling by playing with scale. Scale refers to the comparative size of objects in a space and is so often neglected.

In each and every room I would like to encourage you to add something that is 'too big' into the space. I realize this can sound a bit scary, as it doesn't totally make sense, but you don't create magical spaces by making sense all the time! Adding something supersized gives you instant interior design Brownie points. Upscaling something instantly creates a striking statement (and it's also the easiest thing to do).

When you add something too big to a room, like placing a tall plant on a table, or an oversized artwork on a wall, it is almost like sprinkling everything with fairy dust magic. If everything is perfectly proportioned and just the right size it will read as super boring. When you add something that is too big (no matter the size of your room, bijou or huge) it changes everything in the most enchanting of ways. Pendants that are too large, supersized mirrors, a big sculpture, massive branches from the garden on the centre island, these are all game changing! Then take it one step further and position dainty next to weighty, heavy next to feminine. Nailed it!

When you add a bit of drama to a room it demands to be noticed, just like wearing a cool, swoon-worthy outfit. Look upon introducing scale into a room like you would introduce an exclamation mark into a piece of text. You don't want to litter your space with large pieces, just introduce the odd thing here and there.

This might sound a little contradictory for maximalist interiors but every room needs some negative space. Stimulation and visual friction are great but we also need a breathing space to take stock and regain balance. Negative empty areas allow us to rest our eyes for a second, which subconsciously creates a sense of harmony. An absence, or a space with nothing in it, can make a profound impression (a bit like an eloquent pause in a conversation). You don't need to start rearranging all your furniture – small tweaks have the biggest impact. Consider leaving a breathing space in a cabinet, a little gap on a shelf. It directs attention to the pieces you want to be noticed.

Now let's talk mixing. The most impactful thing you can do to create your maximalist pad is to effortlessly combine furnishings from different periods, styles and of course places. I know this can sound super scary – how do you make it feel cohesive? Fear not, colour is our answer. (A word of warning, I will be saying this a lot!) When you reduce the number of colours in a room to three, maybe four, you can mix anything with anything. It's the easiest way to make a room feel cohesive. Never again will you have to worry, 'Will this go with this?' When you limit the colours you can mix anything. A Chinese dresser next to a contemporary chair, très chic. A fabulous boho vintage lamp next to a modern vase, nice. If you've restricted the colours, it will always work.

Adding something supersized gives you instant interior design Brownie points. Upscaling something instantly creates a striking statement (and it's also the easiest thing to do).

STIMULATION AND VISUAL
FRICTION ARE GREAT BUT
WE ALSO NEED A BREATHING
SPACE TO TAKE STOCK
AND REGAIN BALANCE.
NEGATIVE EMPTY AREAS
ALLOW US TO REST OUR
EYES FOR A SECOND, WHICH
SUBCONSCIOUSLY CREATES
A SENSE OF HARMONY.

Repetition is key in maximalist interiors, regardless of the styles you are mixing. When you repeat colours (or styles or materials), it will feel so much more polished.

I know you're probably thinking at this point that there is a lot to consider, but trust me, once it's part of your natural filter, it gets easier. These rules are very loose. You don't need to specifically adhere to them all, just use them as guidelines.

When you add lots of different materials to your maximalist pad make sure they balance. You wouldn't want a room full of blonde wood tones for example and not much else. So mix things up: brown wood, black wood, matt blonde wood.

Balance glass, metal, velvet, clay. If you can think of your materials in terms of contrasts it will help you create a more layered space.

Odd numbers are pretty intrinsic to interiors, especially maximalist ones. Think of even numbers as creating symmetry and odd numbers as creating interest. Any grouping you have, whether that's a cluster of paintings on a wall, or a group of objects on a shelf, will look so much more interesting if the number of pieces is odd. The reason is that odd numbers make your eye work harder, as it has to move around the grouping and then of course the room. Once the eye starts moving, you up the visual interest. Make sense?

Test it out: if you happen to have a gallery wall that isn't working very well, try a new odd number arrangement. Other combos to try are three cushions on a sofa, three pillows on a bed, five flowers in a vase and of course the classic sofa and two chairs, always a winner.

Would you believe me if I said that the proper arrangement of things can actually make you feel happier? Not just that, but also more intellectually stimulated and engaged? Believe me or not, but when you get a room layout right it actually changes up your space in the most positive of ways and makes you feel happier! All of which nicely segues into my next point – symmetry.

Symmetry can transform the atmosphere in a room. Not to get too psychological on you, but when we walk into a room that feels balanced (and symmetry creates balance), our brains process the room faster as there is less to compute. So balanced rooms feel more aesthetically pleasing. Symmetry is a great way to introduce balance, however a big note of caution: don't overdose. Don't, for example, have two matching bedside tables with two matching lamps on top – that won't make anyone gasp in delight. You could get away with two matching tables, but not two lamps of the same style – that's a big no-no.

You need a little symmetry but not loads, try to avoid the Noah's Ark two-by-two scenario. Symmetry is an easy way to create order because it takes care of the visual balance and will calm things down when there is a lot going on. But don't overdose on multiples. Whenever any of my spaces feel too clustered and 'too much', I introduce a little bit of symmetry. Curtains are often a great way to create the look. When you use symmetry in small doses it will make your space feel far more harmonious, with its instant visual sense. That said, there is such a thing as too much of a good thing, which is why you will also need to shake things up with ASYMMETRY.

Asymmetry is even more of a crucial component to maximalist style than symmetry. With asymmetry a room is balanced by the repetition of similar colours, forms or lines. By this I mean that one side of a sofa could have an occasional table, the other side a floor lamp. When you introduce asymmetry, it lends more visual interest to a space, making it feel more relaxed and cosy. Too much symmetry reads as monotonous, a little formal and to be frank, quite stuffy. Also, with asymmetry, your brain has to work harder reading a room, it's less obvious, so therefore it makes it more interesting. There is clearly a fine balance: too much symmetry is too dull, too much asymmetry is too crazy.

Adopt contradictions and look upon maximalist interiors almost the same way you would look upon a playlist. On my late-night playlist I might have Nina Simone along with Bach, Adele, Leonard Cohen and some Ethiopian jazz. It's not an obvious synchronicity but there is something that all those opposing sounds bring to the table – creating eccentricity and magic. When you combine things from the past with contemporary or post-war pieces it's so much more interesting. Think of yourself as a storyteller, an escapist even, constantly mixing furnishings from disparate eras. It's complex and it's simple at the same time.

One of the easiest ways to start is to look to nature for inspiration. Choosing natural elements that resonate with your personal style is the first step. A dark mahogany bowl perhaps or adding plants and flowers everywhere. Reconnecting with nature revitalizes spaces and adds a whole other layer of serenity into your space. Botanicals are really having their moment, they have gone from being a barely considered accessory to becoming very much the leading lady. You can go large – banana tree anyone? Oversized plants are such an easy way of making a statement without committing to a bold scheme. Or go small with subtle succulents, they are super versatile and will brighten up any surface from the home office to the living room!

Maximalist homes defy trends and are therefore not looking for approval. You need a devil-may-care confidence to pull them off and it's not about how much you spend – these interiors don't count dollars. You're expressing your personality, so trust your own instincts and don't seek out approval from others. Stick to what pleases you. What I happen to love about this style is the freedom that it brings to truly express your passions and personalities. It can tap into something super-interesting and multi-layered.

Creating a sense of 'you' is all about thinking beyond the visual. I want my home to feel metaphorically akin to an embrace. It's why I am constantly banging on about creating a 'feeling' and not a style. When you design rooms around a feeling or an emotion you will get the home of your dreams. If you can blur the lines between practical and beautiful you've nailed it. Everything you select, from the furnishings to the objects, should tell a story. Be confident, be bold and embrace what you love, not just what you feel safe with.

Don't neglect the small things, often it is these that have the most impact. Sentimental pieces you have picked up on far-flung travels, kids' art, or precious cards. When you cluster sentimental pieces with a collection of more serious items you create instant flair. It can help you feel connected and will also bring you comfort. Ceramics, neatly piled books, fluffy pampas grass, dried tree branches, art and statues all sitting side by side. In design it's always the details that count!

Regardless of whether your home is owned or rented, big or small, it's yours. Yours to have fun with and make your own.

When I put my key into the lock after a long day I instantly feel relaxed and cocooned. I feel like the house is giving me the biggest hug. It nourishes me. It feels deliberately tactile as I've created this sensory experience and that in turn has a huge impact on my wellbeing. It's hard to feel happy in a space you're not proud of, so by expressing yourself through your decor, you will always make yourself contented!

When you design rooms around a feeling or an emotion you will get the home of your dreams.

ALL-IMPORTANT ACCESSORIES

Accessories give a room its personality and are the details that turn spaces around. For we maximalists they are essential, because when correctly styled, these showstopping finishing touches make any interior stand out.

From groupings of artful ceramics and clusters of books, to trays, cushions, throws and rugs, accessories create a stimulating sensory home. From botanicals to artworks, these are the details that give spaces energy and provide a narrative about who we are. It is my absolute most favourite part of the decorating process. It's incredible the impact these smaller pieces have on the design, suddenly bringing everything together, as well as enlivening and softening. Adding depth, pattern, texture and colour, it's the details that really are the gateway to creating the most beautiful layered home. I get asked a lot about how to know if a room is incomplete. My answer is to step back, reflect and – as with all creative processes – try to dial into your internal feelings. How do you feel when you walk into the space? Is there anything missing? Is it too bare? Is there enough visual interest going on? Once you can figure out what is lacking, you can build it up from there – and that is where the fun starts. Try things out until you land on a final collection. I don't just whizz into a room, style up a bookcase in a jiffy, and pat myself on the back. I try something; if it doesn't work (and quite often on the first attempt it won't) I'll

try something else, until it does. I'll get as creative as possible, mixing and matching in unusual ways until I land on an arrangement that I love. Before we look more closely at the individual elements I just want to say again that the most important component in knowing when a room is finished is the sensation you get when you enter it. Trust how you feel. It takes time to get it right. Sometimes it's easy, sometimes it takes a lot of trial and error, but when it's right you just know it's right.

We will talk more about the layering process later on, but for now I want to dispel the notion that filling a room with a lot of furniture completes the look. It so doesn't! Accessories help distinguish your home from looking like a furniture showroom; they tell a story of your passions, your travels, your life.

It's the finishing touches that give a room its soul and its energy. Maximalist interiors need to feel spontaneous and actually it's the hardest look to pull off successfully. If they read as too contrived or too perfect, they feel uptight.

One of the tricks is not to plan out every single little thing. When you leave things to chance it can feel more relaxed. Homes should give us joy; step into any one room and our hearts should skip a beat. If yours doesn't, then it's not quite complete. Fear not though, as here are my go-to essential accessories; pieces that I rely on time and time again, that make a house feel like a home.

SOFT FURNISHINGS

Carpets, rugs, upholstery, curtains, cushions, throws – these things give a room such softness and luxury, setting the tone and adding oodles of texture which in turn adds depth and interest. Skimming rugs over hard floors is game-changing, while cushions and throws break up the harsh angles of solid furniture. Not just that, they also add comfort and warmth and help to regulate the acoustics.

Let's start with cushions and throws. I happen to think they are one of the easiest, and in fact cheapest, ways to give your home an instant refresh. Adding cushions and throws helps to bring out the subtle features of a space and if you want to decorate like a pro my biggest tip is to select an anchoring hue. For example, if there is a piece of furniture in your room that brings in a pop of colour make sure the rest of the room highlights it, without outshining it. So in my space, for example, I have soft berry rose pinky accents in a rug, therefore in my cushions and throws I might add in the odd pinky tone. In order to keep things interesting and exciting, however, I also need to introduce a few other hues. I've gone for toffee and cream to accentuate and contrast with the pinky tones.

Remember to mix up the pattern and texture otherwise you won't intrigue the eye and it won't feel engaged. It's so important to add print. If everything is a solid hue it will read as super dull. Don't shy away from experimenting either with prints or shapes. Round cushions break up straight lines, and if you are worried about using print, you can overdose on mixing textures instead. I do this a lot with my throws and cushions – I keep the palette quite restrained but introduce lots of visual interest through texture. You can accessorize with cushions and throws anywhere and everywhere, on sofas and chairs, beds and benches, stools and baskets. Throws can be placed diagonally over the corner of sofas, or, for a more streamlined look, can be folded neatly over the arm. They help break up surfaces, which is why I am so keen on introducing pattern (no matter how subtle).

Balance out the colours and then mix textures for the ultimate in squidgy cosiness. Partner loose weave fabrics like linen with chunky wools, or cashmere with faux fur, the possibilities are endless.

Curtains and blinds have an incredible transformative effect on a room. I especially love adding curtains to small bedrooms and living spaces because if you hang the curtain higher than your window it will instantly emphasize the height of the room and make the space feel taller. Fabric is fundamental when choosing window treatments – too heavy and they won't fold crisply, too light and they might not fall well. When it comes to material, silk, linen, velvet and faux velvet are the best choices as they hang so well. There are so many options with pattern and colour I tend to choose a single shade for both my walls and window coverings. It unifies the scheme, keeping things balanced. It's a trick I use time and time again with paint also, because by using colour in this way your decor becomes almost recessive, allowing all the furniture and accessories to take centre stage – perfect for maximalist interiors. The biggest tip I can give you when selecting curtains and blinds is either to up the texture or up the print, as this will add automatic interest to your scheme. If your curtains have a print, keep the blind behind them a solid hue. Remember large prints and brighter colours draw more attention so are a great option if you want to make your windows the focal point of a room. Solid hues and subtler textures will have a gentler effect, allowing the furnishings to take the spotlight.

Soft furnishings add such a
sumptuousness to a space;
their tactile quality will make
any room feel opulent.

Rugs are one of my most favourite ways of overhauling and refreshing a space, literally from the ground up. They can help to set the tone for an entire space and have an amazing power to transform a room, calming it down or allowing it to take centre stage. I happen to think that every room needs a rug. In my own space, I tend to keep the bedrooms peaceful and restful so I use vintage Berber rugs with a lot of texture. The hallway needs to read as more exciting, so I've introduced a pattern. In the living room I go interesting and patterned, as I need more pizzazz. Having said that though I never want the rug to be the dominant element in the room – I need it to be part of the overall scheme.

There are very few rules with maximalist decorating so don't limit yourself to just one rug in a room. I use multiple rugs that define different areas. Particularly in large spaces multiple rugs will help to ground disparate groupings of furniture. You can also layer rugs on top of each other: large plainer ones on the bottom and smaller decorative ones on top. One trick is to go for a relatively inexpensive plain rug (like a natural sisal) and then layer softer, plusher kilims or dhurries on top.

It's such a personal choice, whether you opt for pattern or go more understated. Whichever route you take, know that it will add instant warmth and interest to any room.

When thinking about soft furnishings, my advice is to balance out the colours and then mix textures for the ultimate in squidgy cosiness. Partner loose-weave fabrics like linen with chunky wools, or cashmere with faux fur, the possibilities are endless. Working with a restrained colour scheme is the easiest way to layer – it's cohesive and calming. Soft furnishings add such a sumptuousness to a space; their tactile quality will make any room feel opulent.

ORNAMENTS AND ARTWORKS

Decorative accessories leave an instant impression, whether in the form of trays or candles, framed photos or books. When you fill rooms with things that you love you will feel happy every time you enter. Use trays everywhere from your kitchen island to your coffee table. They are great for putting multiple objects on but, even better, can be used to corral accessories on a table surface and lend a sense of organization to decorative vignettes. This is super important for maximalist spaces – when you put multiple pieces on a tray it instantly feels more stylized and therefore less cluttered.

Books are a great way of humanizing spaces, whether you stack them on ottomans, coffee tables and mantelpieces or layer them up in bookcases and shelves, they are the easiest way to add warmth and texture to a space. In maximalist interiors books are an important decorative statement. You can group by colour and size or mix them all up. Anything like a bookcase needs breaking up with more personalized decorative touches in among all the tomes; think art, vases or anything you happen to collect. Don't get hung up with aligning books, interrupt them with paintings, photos or bowls. Every table in my pad houses a little cluster of books so my home library isn't just restricted to the shelves – I dot books all over. Books help set a mood and decorating with them is one of the easiest and perhaps most stylish ways of instantly upgrading your space.

Mirrors expand horizons, add depth and bring an instant decorative touch, and as such, every maximalist interior needs a mirror. Their reflections make a room feel larger than it actually is. When selecting a mirror don't feel confined in your frame choices. Curly flourishes, round, rectangular, gilded, it matters not. A trick I use time and time again is to supersize them, going for slightly larger than feels comfortable. It works on so many levels – not only does it make the room feel grander, it also opens up the space beautifully, giving it the optical illusion of more depth and more intrigue. Conventional wisdom is one mirror per room, but I have four in my living room alone! Not all of them are large but every one of them has changed it around. When in doubt, add a mirror on top of cabinets, as a backsplash, or at the end of a hallway. Mirrors add glamour, make a niche sparkle and create the illusion of depth.

Often considered the last buy, long after the paint has dried, artworks embellish spaces like nothing else I know. One of the most basic principles of interior design is that every room has to have a focal point. (I happen to think that rooms need more than one focal but more on that later.) Focal points draw the eye into the space and make a room feel more magical. Pieces of art act as an instant focal point. You can turn stark, bare walls into stylish centrepieces – I like to go supersized a lot of the time as this commands instant attention and sets the tone.

Gallery walls displaying collections of photographs, art, ephemera, wall hangings and kids' art add instant personality. When you hang multiple pieces in a group, visual balance is very important, particularly with maximalist spaces as otherwise it can feel super messy. Position the most prominent piece in the centre at eye level and work outward. If using different frames spread them out to give a little breathing space between each piece.

If your decor is quite loud then the art you choose should not be quite so flamboyant or it can feel overpowering (and vice versa). Think about balance. One bold, over-the-top piece can read as kitsch, whereas one too-simple piece can read as unconnected. Be strategic about colour palettes and think about balancing everything. I tend to steer away from bold blingy hues (totally personal), as I don't want any one thing commanding all the attention. I like to connect my art with a controlled collection of colours, this really adds decorum, I feel. Art is, of course, such a great reflection of your personality so there really is no wrong or no right.

I also love overlapping artworks, layering them up and propping things on a mantle or fireplace – this sets a relaxed vibe and makes a house feel like a home. Take it one step further and prop a frame on the floor for an even more relaxed, casual vibe. When it comes to where to place art – anywhere and everywhere I say! Living rooms, hallways and bedrooms are obvious options but I would encourage unexpected areas also, like kitchens, landings, toilets and bathrooms. When it comes to how many pieces, as always, listen to your intuition.

MAXIMALISM MEANS MORE OF
EVERYTHING: MORE OF WHAT
YOU LOVE, MORE OF YOUR
FAVOURITE HUES, ACCESSORIES
AND FABRICS. RESTRICT
THE COLOURS, REIN IN THE
PATTERNS, CONSTANTLY REPEAT
AND THEN EVERYTHING WILL
FEEL COHESIVE.

Fragrance

Scents are accessories too, adding such character to a home, and yet often neglected. These are my own personal favourites.

→ For living rooms I like soft background scents: masculine scents like tobacco or cedarwood and earthy notes like musk.

→ For dining rooms I like delicate aromas that don't overpower food, refreshing scents like lemon verbena. Coriander is a good one for kitchens – a lovely, warming scent.

→ In bedrooms I plump for scents formulated with notes of Nordic woods and blackened oak – calming and restorative. Sandalwood and mint are fab for bathrooms.

I buy pot pourri from Santa Maria Novella – the oldest pharmacy in Italy. I decant it into tea light holders and scatter them everywhere.

PLANTS AND FLOWERS

As a great way to bring a space to life and add warmth and intrigue, I often use flowers and plants in place of other decorative accessories, whether a single stem or a grouping. They add colour, shape and texture and are surprisingly versatile. Mix shiny with pointy, feathery with glossy and matt. I am a little foliage obsessed; different leaves and textures add such interesting layers. Don't overlook branches, berries and ferns – on their own or en masse.

There's a movement afoot in flowers and it's one that I am super excited about. It's a natural offshoot of the trend towards eating seasonally – foraged flora in all stages of life is beginning to take centre stage. That includes weeds, roadside foliage and branches, they are all having a moment. It sets such a relaxed, naturalistic vibe, and is a big move away from overly styled 'dome' arrangements. Now it's much more about being freeform and loose. Decorating with nature and bringing the beauty of the changing seasons into your home is easy and inexpensive and the materials are on our doorsteps. I have fireplaces in each and every room so I've always got baskets filled with wood which lend a warm and cosy vibe. Branches in vases are always a must for me – in spring I add blossoms, in winter bare fig branches – to bring interest to my hallway and dining table. Boughs and organic materials add such an authentic and earthy touch to any home.

OCCASIONAL FURNITURE

You can elevate virtually any room with occasional accent pieces like stools, benches and little tables. Decorative and functional in equal measure, if your room feels lacking in any way these pieces of furniture will certainly do the trick, setting the tone for the rest of the space. They are the best way to add a new silhouette, a new style or to introduce a new colour.

When it comes to little chairs, you can mix in pairs making up a cosy nook, or they are an ideal companion next to a sofa or by the side of a bed, prettying up the space. Lightweight and easy to move around, occasional chairs are great pieces to have in your maximalist arsenal. Plonk them anywhere and everywhere and they will give a room a sense of place and also ground it. I think their ability to fit in anywhere is why they are so popular in maximalist interiors, from landings to alcoves. You can accessorize with a heap of books or leave unadorned.

Benches are another great decorating tool: sitting in front of a sofa, at the end of the bed, or skimming a hallway. These long, low-slung and extremely beautiful seats can be found in every style; retro, modern, traditional, cushioned or firm, dressed up or dressed down. Ends of beds and hallways are obvious places for them but there are so many others, from flanking a dining table to using them for transitional spaces like between a kitchen and living area, for example. Whether serving as the perfect accent piece or for squeezing in extra guests at dinner, a bench's double-duty ability makes it one of the most hardworking pieces out there.

Smaller accent side tables are just as crucial to a space as, say, your coffee table or sofa – they really finish a space off, from providing a surface to rest a drink on to showcasing your design aesthetic. There are so many options when it comes to materials. For a casual laid-back vibe opt for jute, bamboo or wood or go metal and reflective if you want to rock a more glamorous sensibility. They are such an important decorative tool, not only catching all the day's miscellany – books, glasses and everything in between – they also add one of those all-important layers.

Lightweight and easy to move around, occasional chairs are great pieces to have in your maximalist arsenal. Plonk them anywhere and everywhere and they will give a room a sense of place and also ground it.

PRIVATE

When it comes to accessorizing a room, it's important to consider everything as a whole. Too many colours can read as jarring, too many one-dimensional textures as too flat. What makes or breaks a space is not each individual piece but the combination of pieces and how they work together in a room. Our maximalist rooms need to feel polished not messy, finished not cluttered. There is such a fine line between fearless mishmash and stop-you-in-your-tracks beauty that enthrals and excites. Through the accessories you choose you can create real visual theatre.

By all means mix colours, but mix within the same family – it means you can mix more and add more! When in doubt and if the room starts to feel too full-on, add anchoring accessories in black and neutrals, they will break everything up and this will give you more freedom with your mixing.

THE BEST THING ABOUT
ACCESSORIZING IN A
MAXIMALIST WAY IS
THAT YOU GET TO CREATE
A MULTI-SENSORY
WONDERLAND.

If you are new to maximalism I suggest starting small and building up from there. Begin by accessorizing hallways, guest rooms, breakfast nooks and bathrooms. They are great spaces to dip your toe in, outside of your comfort zone. Because they are rooms that you are often in and out of, you will almost feel freer to create drama.

I've mentioned this before, but I'll say it again here, symmetry helps achieve order in maximalist rooms, so when it comes to accessories you will find you can successfully layer far more if you constantly think about balance (and symmetry creates balance). You'll know if you've overdone it on the symmetry front if you can no longer see a definitive composition.

Maximalism means more of everything: more of what you love, more of your favourite hues, accessories and fabrics. Restrict the colours, rein in the patterns, constantly repeat and then everything will feel cohesive. The best thing about accessorizing in a maximalist way is that you get to create a multi-sensory wonderland.

97

IDENTIFYING YOUR PALETTE

Colour is the single most transformative, game-changing trick you can perform. Get it right and it lifts your spirits and your energy levels – lively reds or joyful yellows anyone? Get it wrong and it instantly makes you run for the hills! Dramatically daring hues go hand in glove with maximalist interiors but you can also create a beautiful home with softer colours.

I am so drawn to the notion of surrounding yourself with colours that you love. Colours that aren't necessarily on trend, hot or cool, but instead resonate with the heart.

Colour is emotional, as we all respond to it differently and it has this incredible ability not only to transform a space but add certain evocations of emotion. Clever, right?

Each and every colour has its very own psychological value so ensure that you select hues that make you feel good. Start by asking yourself how you want to feel in your space. Calm and relaxed? Lively with a bit of contrast? Snug perhaps? Harmonious? I, for instance, adore deep, inky bottom-of-the-lake hues. Hushed, deeply saturated tones that are intense, timeless and sophisticated. Earthy, deeply complex colours that are impactful as they exaggerate cosiness, giving me a home I never what to leave. BUT place me in a Wes Anderson-esque candyfloss-pink interior and I'll be reaching for the whisky in next to no time!

Maximalist interiors pile on the colour but don't think you have to go full-on bold canary yellow, tomato red or sky blue to pull this look off. Yes, maximalism adores vibrancy, but it also likes harmony. My biggest tip when selecting a colour palette is to make it personal. If you can, try to think outside of the box rather than playing it safe, as your room will be far more tantalizing. Playing it safe results in rooms that read as visually flat and uninspiring.

One thing when it comes to colour selection: never get caught up with trends as they come and go. You can only make a home beautiful by selecting colours that reflect your personality and are your own preferences, not what some magazine or paint company deems as being on trend. The trick, obviously, is to blend the colours you love into pleasing combinations. When you get it right that combo becomes your secret formula, allowing you to create the most magical of spaces. Aspirational, inspirational, cocooning, energizing – how clever is colour!

Don't compromise or play it too safe. I've heard so many times from my students that walls should be kept neutral in case somewhere down the line the house is resold – why for potential prospective buyers do walls have to stay dull? Or that they've selected a neutral sofa over an inky blue one because it felt more practical. The trouble with avoiding colour and worrying about mistakes is that playing it safe will make your home look and feel more boring. One of the biggest mistakes of all is sitting on the fence and doing nothing. I get that colour can feel scary, but we maximalists like taking risks!

Shop your own clothing – it will instantly tell you which colours you gravitate towards. As Coco Chanel so succinctly put it, 'The best colour in the world is the one that looks good on you.' Your wardrobe makes a great starting point; if I look at mine it's peppered with full-on noirs, toffees, pink-brown undertones, with some neutrals – all the same colours that I've used throughout my home.

What I find so fascinating is that the colour in a room can have a direct impact on how you feel – so choose wisely. Think about how certain colours affect you, do they energize or relax you? Work out what mood you want to create in each room and how colour will help you achieve that.

Colour has the power to change the size of a room, it can make it feel grander, or cooler. If you are in a conundrum look at magazines, books and Pinterest and let your heart be your guide.

One of the biggest mistakes of all is sitting on the fence and doing nothing. I get that colour can feel scary, but we maximalists like taking risks!

SHOP YOUR OWN CLOTHING –
IT WILL INSTANTLY TELL YOU
WHICH COLOURS YOU GRAVITATE
TOWARDS. AS COCO CHANEL SO
SUCCINCTLY PUT IT, 'THE BEST
COLOUR IN THE WORLD IS THE
ONE THAT LOOKS GOOD ON YOU.

Once you've happened upon a selection you like, try to limit the number of hues in a room – ideally no more than three, possibly four. Repeat these colours throughout, it will give your space extra kudos and make the scheme read as far more cohesive. Echo the colours in rugs, vases and lamps. This will create instant harmony, balance and cohesion.

Too many colours can make a room feel too busy – getting this right takes a little bit of experimentation, but stick with it. When figuring out your palette I would encourage you, rather than playing it safe, to push slightly out of your comfort zone and be brave.

Start small, you don't need to repaint all your walls instantly or have every single soft furnishing in a bold hue. Decorating with colour can seem super-scary if your default is pale, but try to brush aside these fears. Start by introducing colour in the smallest of ways, like in a vase, a throw, or some candles. It will elevate, uplift and pack a visual punch. The more confident you get, the bigger and bolder you can take it. Until you've dabbled you have no idea how life-changing it can really be. Colour can make the heart skip a beat. It makes you feel, braver, bolder and more kick-ass in your approach to life and to living – promise!

Once you've got the bug, I would encourage any maximalist to start selecting a colour palette for the whole house rather than choosing colours on an as-needed basis. This can cause quite a lot of stress and indecisiveness, not to mention the odd room (or rooms) feeling disjointed from the rest if you don't consider the space as whole. Every space, no matter if it's open plan or a series of rooms, needs a considered palette. There is a lot going on in maximalist interiors so you don't want to turn a corner and have a jarring feeling because the colour hasn't quite worked.

When figuring out your palette I would encourage you, rather than playing it safe, to push slightly out of your comfort zone.

107

More importantly, you want to create connection between rooms or areas, so as you transition through the space, rooms are not a series of snapshots or a jumbly mess of stuff with a hodge-podge of different colours going on. Instead you want every room in your house to feel that it's from the same house. Start with the room you spend the most time in, like the living room, and then co-ordinate, harmonize and blend out from there. Create simple harmonies between rooms, relating them to one another. Concentrate particularly on the social spaces of the home – the living room, kitchen and dining room are all key. You don't have to make them the same colour, just make sure you are creating this subconscious feeling of continuity.

A quick note about colour temperature... all colours have a temperature and depending on where they fall on the colour wheel are either cool or warm. For example, reds, oranges and yellows are warm and in contrast blues and purples are cool. Visually warm colours appear to advance, as do dark colours, which is why they are often used to make spaces feel cosier, more cocooning and more intimate. The opposing theory works for cool colours, typified by colours such as blues, greens and light purples – they calm and soothe and appear to recede. One word of warning though, please don't think you can paint a small room out in a cool pale tone and suddenly it will look and feel a million times bigger, because it won't. I happen to think that if you paint a small room out in a dark hue your eye forgets how small it is and only focuses on how cool it is!

WORKING WITHIN A FRAMEWORK

Now we need to analyse any fixed elements, like hardwood floors, brick walls, or stone countertops for instance, although don't worry about trim or cabinetry because that can all easily be painted out. Then we start building the palette. I'll give you an example: the flooring in my lower ground floor is concrete so therefore a cool grey in hue. I wanted the paint colour to have warmer tones in the kitchen and den area so choose a burnt caramel, almost caramelized toffee, hue. A lovely contrast to the cooler grey floor.

Most of my fixed elements – like the concrete floor and black stone worktops – have cool undertones, therefore when it comes to painting the walls it's quite exciting to contrast them with warmer colours. When you contrast, it can make things feel far more harmonious and interesting.

Another tip – if you're not keen on your flooring, don't panic, it's an easy fix. I have orangish pine floorboards on all my other floors apart from the bathroom, original to my 1860s London townhouse. I hated them when varnished so instead simply painted them out in the same hue as the walls, and then they immediately disappeared. If you have tile and hate it, or vinyl and detest it, you can so easily skim with rugs and then base your palette from the ground up with your new covering.

When you contrast, it can make things feel far more harmonious and interesting.

108

YOUR PERSONAL COLOUR SCHEME

When it comes to identifying your colour palette, start with working out the overall feeling you want to create in your home. Once you've figured out the feeling you want to achieve you can then look for inspiration everywhere and anywhere: nature, fashion, fabrics, the Internet.

There is a lot to consider when figuring out your colour scheme. Will it work? Is it going to look good? Are you going to hate it? When in doubt, reference the colour wheel – pro designers follow it all the time and it can help guide you. There are so many colour schemes to choose from but I'm going to focus on the three main ones: monochromatic, analogous and complementary.

→ You don't see very many **monochromatic schemes** in maximalist interiors because this one-hue scheme – where the entire palette is based around a single colour and then builds interest through different shades, tones and tints of that colour – can sometimes be considered boring. Don't think of it as using one single shade, instead you are choosing a base colour plus any number of variations on that base. For example, let's say I'm going green: I'll vary the saturation levels from forest greens to limes, pears, shamrocks, sea foams, olives to emeralds. Or how about browns? There are so many variants: buff, chestnut, burnt umber, desert sand, chocolate. See where I am going with this? Working the single colour look is so easy and when you go up and down the saturation level it feels so much more complex! Everything feels harmonious and visually cohesive – this palette lets the pieces in your place shine, as it doesn't draw too much attention to itself. It can (and does) simplify a design if everything is feeling too busy and too confusing. The disadvantages are that it's super restrictive and it lacks contrast. You can't suddenly throw in a dollop of chartreuse to liven things up. Just remember to get creative with texture and finishes so that they contrast and complement.

→ An **analogous colour scheme**, often referred to as a **harmonious scheme**, uses colours adjacent to each other on the colour wheel, so usually involves three hues all of which are positioned next to each other. Technically speaking, analogous colour schemes have one dominant colour (usually a primary or secondary colour), then a supporting colour (normally a secondary or tertiary colour) and then a third colour, which is either a mix of the two first colours or an accent. Make sense? You can add neutrals to this scheme to balance it all or use this scheme for your accent hues. Some combos: blue, green and blue-green are beautiful; or how about violet, red-violet, and red, which is a little more daring but still super cool?

→ **Complementary colours** are those that sit directly opposite each other on the colour wheel. It's the most energetic of the three schemes because it's all about contrast, so it reads as super lively. Typically one colour acts as the dominant shade and the others as the accents. Think greens with reds, or oranges with blues. Add in neutrals as they provide a place for the eye to rest and keep things from becoming overwhelming.

I AM SO DRAWN TO THE NOTION
OF SURROUNDING YOURSELF
WITH COLOURS THAT YOU
LOVE. COLOURS THAT AREN'T
NECESSARILY ON TREND,
HOT OR COOL, BUT INSTEAD
RESONATE WITH THE HEART.

There are other schemes out there if you want to get more complicated. For example, a **triadic scheme** uses three colours with equal space between them on the wheel. A tetradic structure is sometimes referred to as a **rectangular scheme** because of the shape it makes on the wheel – it focuses on using two distinct pairs of complementary colours.

Don't get too hung up with the colour wheel, just know that it's a good tool to refer to if you find yourself in a conundrum. It removes all the guesswork and gives you an instant visual representation of what works and blends nicely together.

Colour is personal, so don't worry too much about following the rules. However, I tend to think that the most successful rooms keep colours within the same tonal family, as too many strong hues can be overwhelming for the senses.

When it comes to figuring out your colour palette, start with working out the overall feeling you want to create in your home.

BRINGING COLOUR IN

Colour can be incorporated in so many ways, from accessories to big bold statements on walls. I love maximalist interiors but you won't see lots of clashing garish colours going on in my pad. Garish and maximalism are not mutually inclusive. Choose colours that work with the mood you are trying to create. Not all colours are created equally and will project different feelings depending on their hue. For example, reds are fiery and high energy. Good for a home office perhaps but not a bedroom that might need something a little more calming, such as greens, pinks or browns. I like using yellow accents in the kitchen, whether that's in flowers or on a vase, as it's so bright and cheery – and this room is where we all officially wake up and start our day.

Often, maximalist interiors get tarnished with being over-stimulating with their bold, crazy, cool colours. It's important to find a middle ground with colour – a place where bold colours can stand out – but also we need to provide a place for the eye to rest, which is where neutrals come in. Luckily there is an easy trick out there that lots of designers reference: it's called the 60/30/10 rule.

Many interior designers the world over embrace this rule, as it ensures a visually appealing, balanced interior. How does it work? So, under this rule, 60 per cent of your space will be the base colour, another 30 per cent the accent hue, and then 10 per cent the pop of colour. I've whittled it down for you even further. Walls, area rugs, and large furniture are your 60 per centers. Occasional chairs, window treatments, bedding and rugs your 30 per centers and finally cushions, throws, art and accessories the 10 per centers!

You can, of course, go rogue and break the rules to create your own formula. Be rebellious – how about 30/30/20/20 perhaps? Whatever feels right for you, just pay attention to the balance in your space and be aware of the visual impact.

When choosing colour schemes for your maximalist home bear in mind that complementary colour schemes tend to make a room feel more crisp and arresting and analogous ones more relaxing.

Decorating with colour can seem super scary if your default is pale, but try to brush aside these fears. Start by introducing colour in the smallest of ways, like in a vase, a few cushions or some candles. It will elevate, uplift and pack a visual punch.

FOUR TIPS THAT WILL CHANGE THE WAY YOU DECORATE WITH COLOUR

1. **Take a colour and put it on repeat**. Consistently and always repeat.

2. **Buddy up with neutrals**. If everything feels too OTT in a space, befriend neutrals. Neutrals have magical powers – they can freshen up a space, or dial it down and they always look polished, sophisticated and welcoming.

3. **There is no official limit to how many colours you can have in a room**. The way to know if you've got it right is to start paying attention to each colour you've used and eliminate elements until the room feels balanced.

4. **Colours create a visual story**, so if your space feels too predictable and too repetitive, fix it by adding in a handful of colours that have nothing to do with the palette. This will infuse the space with life.

The biggest way that I can help you when it comes to choosing colour is to advise you to follow your heart. Ditch restrictions, banish hidden voices like 'Can your small room take a dark hue?' (Yes it can). 'Can a south-facing room be painted in a warm hue?' (Yes it can). Follow your heart and not your head and don't discuss it with anybody. Friends, family, decorators – they all get super scared when colour is discussed and will try to put you off and make you put the brakes on.

Darks and Lights

Dramatic, elegant and capable of making any room feel uber sophisticated, chic and timeless, dark hues are my absolute obsession. Swampy, inky colours that make spaces feel super-seductive and are deeply complex – they give a room soul! They are synonymous with mystery as corners blur out and spaces feel magical. Dark colours transmit a powerful message of coolness and exaggerate cosiness like nothing else I know. In dark rooms it's important to create contrast as well as a sense of balance, so overdose on textures like wood, metal, rattan, velvet or leather and introduce lighter and bolder colours – they will really pop.

Taupes, khakis, rain cloud greys and sands are all easy on the eye, perfect for colourphobes and will really help out maximalist interiors. Don't think of them as boring – create contrast by mixing up the texture. Offset rough with soft; shiny with matt; coarse with smooth. Neutrals are a potent player in the game of manipulating a space. They never get too loud or abrasive. Wispy, cool, aloof, warm or welcoming, you don't need crazy colour to make rooms feel and look lively.

Decorating with colour can be intimidating and I know so many people are colour adverse. If you are new to colour, start small: a shot of bright colour on a wall for instance, or some colourful accessories turn things around. Always remember to offset with neutrals and constantly repeat colours back. Like everything with decorating, in order to make your space feel cohesive and beautiful, you have to put things constantly on repeat. If it feels like too much of a conundrum, get to know the colour wheel a little (page 111). You'll see how some colours work naturally together while others clash. As a rule, complementary hues (those that sit opposite each other on the wheel) always work. Alternatively, pick colours either side of your main colour and work within tones. I am a big fan of dialling tones up and down, which gives me so much variety. For example, I might have a pale summer-cloud grey painted on the walls, but then a deep stormy

charcoal rug on the floor with the odd lilac-grey accessory thrown in. It's all about the combos and the more you deep dive into colour the more obsessed you will get.

If you restrict the number of colours in your maximalist scheme you will get a far cooler effect. So pick your palette and put it on repeat. Working with a streamlined palette not only makes rooms feel cohesive it also helps the transitions between rooms. Case in point: when you're in the middle of my hallway (painted an inky brown), you're able to see into my studio, which is dark black, as well as over the balcony to downstairs, painted out in an inky grey-green. It feels so grounding yet each room is individual. The hues vary but the saturation level stays the same.

If you build a timeless foundation with your palette you've nailed it. Watching everything come together is both astonishing and delightful – life-enhancing actually. Surround yourself with colours that you love and your home will always be happy.

CREATING A SENSE OF HOME

Maximalist style is all about being a mixologist and a collector of things – and this certainly applies to furniture. From old antique dressers to mid-century lamps, it's about conversational pieces that delight the eye. The most impactful spaces are ones that effortlessly combine furnishings from different periods, different styles and different places.

Such spaces read as multi-faceted and multi-layered. Stimulating and sensory, it's the visual cacophony of pieces picked up from far-flung travels, flea markets, the high street, galleries or even the shop on the corner that make these non-conformist spaces come alive. Pieces that tell a narrative tantalize and intrigue the senses and make for the coolest spaces around. They inspire in a way that minimalism just can't. Nothing is there simply for the sake of being there – every element is impressive in its own right.

This takes a little bit of skill, as it's super important for maximalist interiors to feel curated as opposed to messy. You'll need a big dose of confidence and a penchant for mixing unexpected pieces together, but it's actually easier than you might think. I know it can feel a tad overwhelming if you've never dabbled with mixing before but fear not as there are all sorts of tricks out there that will make it easier.

Know this – by effortlessly combining elements together in the most intriguing of ways, you will completely turn your home around. Look at it a bit like holding a dinner party with a whole host of different guests from diverse places around the globe, all of varying ages, all with varying interests. Intriguing, right?

It's not as difficult as it may sound. Here are some foolproof decorating tips to help you start thinking like a mixologist when it comes to combining furniture styles.

→ Create as much friction and tension between pieces as possible (see pages 52–56). The trick is to establish sensations between external surfaces that are opposing and not similar, that way it is far more tantalizing. So you wouldn't, for instance, pair a shiny metal table next to a glossy metal chair on a lustrous concrete floor or have a room full of mid-brown wood tones. That's way too one-dimensional. Instead you might want to marry marble with rattan, black with blonde, glass with wood, metal with velvet – the more you contrast, the cooler it gets. Remember rough textures make spaces feel more intimate and grounded while smooth textures bring a sleeker more sophisticated vibe to the space – we need both of course, as contrast keeps things balanced and provides interest. If everything were too similar it would read like a big yawn!

→ The most successful spaces always have some common ground and therefore link, not necessarily in style, but in silhouette, material, colour or form, so make sure there are some connections. There are two ways to go: you can co-ordinate and harmonize so you're blending shapes, tones, patterns or you can purposely contrast, as we've just discussed. When you add contrast you are freely and intentionally unbalancing things. This is what I do a lot, and this is what creates the friction I am looking for. Partner a Chinese screen next to a 1950s table and watch the space come alive. A modern chair beside an 18th-century dresser, or a Parisian lamp next to an old, ornately carved Indian cabinet. The shot of unpredictability is what enlivens rooms.

→ Comfort is a recurring theme in maximalist interiors, whether you're mixing classical design with the clean lines of modernity or the simple silhouette of something mid-century; anything goes as long as it reads as comfortable.

→ What's especially important is to distribute furniture pieces equally, and so many people get this wrong. Go too heavy-handed with one style and a room can feel off balance. Or if one half rocks a mid-century vibe and the other half has nothing mid-century in it at all, the difference is too overwhelming. Look at a room strategically – think about placement and think about balance.

So, any and all styles work in maximalist spaces, and in fact, sticking to one style of furniture is probably the biggest no-no ever. I would encourage you to mix from at least three different time periods if you can. It's then you get to create a really interesting and dynamic space. Don't get too caught up in the trap of following a specific trend – say, Scandi, mid-century or traditional (see pages 29–30) – just go with what you love. That way you create multi-layered spaces which are more about your personal style and will therefore be unique.

When mixing multiple styles, it's best to figure out which style is the dominant one. Take my place, for example, where I have this grit-with-glam, tribal sensibility threaded throughout. I lean slightly more towards the glamorous side than the grittier, edgier side and then the tribal side is the one that I'll pepper in last. It's crucial that not every furniture style is fighting for attention. I need a leader, a dominating design, otherwise my space will read like a hot mess. Different styles work so much better together and will not fight against each other if they are all assigned definitive roles from the get-go.

Ask yourself continually which styles appeal to you and why. Is it the shapes, the colours, the textures, the silhouettes? Drilling down into these reasons will allow you to tie pieces from different styles together.

Different styles work so much better together and will not fight against each other if they are all assigned definitive roles from the get-go.

134

TEXTURE

The mixing of textures is fundamental in maximalist spaces. When you are blending furniture styles, texture is a powerful tool that will unite and harmonize or contrast and stand out. Think about every single texture in your room, from coarse to smooth, from shaggy rugs to roughly hewn pots, metallic bowls or glass lamps. Everything has a texture of course, but I am talking about pieces with surfaces that stand out from their surroundings so they have a real tactile quality.

You can blend textures and mix textures – it all adds another layer of intrigue for the eye. Texture is so under-considered. You can use it to turn a space around in seconds. If your space feels dull it's so easy to switch up. Let's say your velvet sofa feels rather lacking. Opt for woollen cushions, metallic leather cushions and fluffy sheepskin throws – this will provide friction between the surfaces. And don't forget the all-important repetition. You need to use one texture at least three times for a space to be cohesive. If you are consistent with texture it will help your decor hang out together far more happily.

MATERIALS

The same attention should be applied to materials.
For instance, you don't want to end up with a
room full of grey tones, from a grey concrete floor
to a grey ceramic coffee table. Instead mix wood in
with the sleek concrete (or marble, or travertine).
Throw in more rustic materials like rattan and
cane. Go shiny with finishes, and then go matt.
Add in glass, mix in velvets and mohairs. Even
wood grain can be contrasted or harmonized. In
general, larger wood grains read as more casual
while finer grains signal formality. I like to mix
both. Wood has such a warm feel to it. With
its rich tones and variety of finishes it makes
any interior instantly cosy. When you think of
materials always think to contrast – it will so help
you create a layered, interesting space.

Think of a cityscape where you have a plethora of verticals and a lively rhythm of lines that take the eye up and bring the eye down. We need to do the very same thing with our interiors.

SCALE

Proportion and scale have the power to make rooms feel welcoming, magical and inviting. If everything in a space is the same size and the same scale it can feel like your room has just come straight out of the pages of a catalogue – super boring. So variety is definitely key. Make sure you introduce lots of different sizes and scales in terms of items, like tables and upholstered pieces – you will delight, intrigue and tantalize everyone including yourself.

Think of a cityscape where you have a plethora of verticals and a lively rhythm of lines that take the eye up and bring the eye down. We need to do the very same thing with our interiors. Always group items with different heights and shapes together. Keeping everything a similar height looks flat, so combine tall with short, and skinny with plump to create visual interest.

Now play around with proportion – if everything is perfectly proportioned your room can seem quite formal. Try putting a really large vessel on a small table, or a small chair next to a larger table. It will give your room an exclamation mark, a bit of theatre. Oh, and before anyone says it doesn't make sense, that is actually the point. We do not want to make sense. 'Go big or go home' is what I say. Oversized pieces act as focal points and create a buzz without making a room feel too busy. Scale is actually one of the most under-considered components in the decorating puzzle. Don't be scared about playing around with it. Putting dainty furniture pieces such as little chairs next to heavier, weightier coffee tables, for instance, looks beautiful. Suspending a large pendant low over a table, fabulous. These grand gestures make rooms mesmerizing.

PIECES THAT TELL A NARRATIVE
TANTALIZE AND INTRIGUE THE
SENSES AND MAKE FOR THE
COOLEST SPACES AROUND.
THEY INSPIRE IN A WAY THAT
MINIMALISM JUST CAN'T.

TYING THINGS TOGETHER

The easiest way to bring coherence to a room with a variety of furniture styles in it is to limit the colour palette. When you work with a restrained, restricted palette your space will always read as beautiful and harmonious. Colour is the best unifier ever and limiting the palette creates the best cohesion between pieces. With so many different styles going on it's easy for rooms to seem messy and cluttered. Yet you can make everything feel effortlessly curated, cohesive and unified simply by restraining the palette. Too many colours can detract from the overall feeling, so if you are selective – no matter the variations in furniture style – your home will always feel beautiful. I tend to go for three to four colours per room and then I vary and connect them throughout by including a shade's close family members. Don't be afraid to go with your instincts: ignore trends and what's hot right now and follow your heart instead.

Repetition is fundamental in maximalist spaces, making them feel more polished, considered and curated. When are you mixing different furniture styles it's really important to repeat. This applies to colours, materials, forms – I often bring in consistency by focusing on the lines of a particular piece of furniture, like a sofa, say, then repeating the curve throughout my space in a chair, stool or vase, for instance.

In terms of materials, I'll often try to tie in the same shades of wood. If I have a lot of wooden pieces in a room rather than everything being a totally different tone, I prefer to keep it all quite similar. I often plump for hardwoods like walnut, mango or cocobolo which are darker in colour than softwoods. This means that my vintage carved dresser from India (made from mango wood) looks beautiful next to my wenge side table. Both have dense, dark black-brown tones – fabulous!

Go rogue! I always like to introduce a piece of furniture that doesn't relate in any way to anything else, so is an 'oddball' piece, if you like. It draws the eye and acts as an additional focal point. In maximalist interiors, unlike any other style, it's best to have three focal points in a room, to keep things interesting.

The Mighty Chair

I am chair obsessed. They effortlessly pull rooms together and good ones are chic and timeless. If your space is lacking a focal point, or feels a little off, consider adding in this mighty piece of furniture. From deep, comfy occasional armchairs with plush seating to something more lightweight, you can never have too many chairs. You can add formality, or go for more of a casual vibe. When you mix opulent and upholstered with sleek, rugged and worn something amazing happens. I have chairs everywhere, from landings to alcoves.

It's a little harder when it comes to dining chairs to mix in such a freehand way, as 6–10 mismatched chairs around a table can look super messy. This is quite a tricky look to pull off, so I tend to mix in pairs. And, as much as I'm all for a lively rhythm of heights around a room, I think when it comes to dining chairs the seat height and backs need to be similar otherwise it can feel a little disjointed. Give each piece some companions that share a colour, style or finish. Matching lines and shapes will help to unify everything.

Placement is key when mixing furniture styles in maximalist interiors. Ask yourself, how closely are the disparate furnishings going to be together? Sometimes you might want them to butt up to each other but then if they are all bunched up they might not look as cool as if they were on opposite sides of the room. I tend to do a bit of both: in order for different styles to hold their own I need space around them – that way they take far more prominence. Having said that, I'll also group, let's say, a little seating arrangement together, with some lamps and a few occasional tables.

When it comes to furniture, although you can mix almost any styles together, some combinations will work better than others. For example, super traditional partnered with rustic is quite hard to make look right. But contemporary with rustic? Beautiful. Anything Asian is so easy and so beautiful to mix with contemporary pieces, creating a unique look. With antiques it's the same – it's that tension between modern and antique that creates magic. It might sound scary now but the more you adopt contradictions the cooler your space will look. For example, want your bedroom to be a mix of French Provençal with mid-century staples and some contemporary art? Go for it. Want to mix marbleized wallpaper with a powder blue sofa? Try it! Things that don't obviously pair well together often make for the most interesting interiors.

It might sound scary now but the more you adopt contradictions the cooler your space will look.

FURNITURE PLACEMENT

One of the most important things to consider when arranging furniture is traffic flow. You can draw a floor plan, make a sketch, cut out scaled pieces of furniture of paper – the list goes on and on – but to get the flow right I do it intuitively. Leave me in a room for a while and I'll happily move and push things into place, working out my traffic lanes. Give it a try. Don't get too caught up in it, just make sure there is enough room to pass through without tripping over everything. You'll need a flow around the room and around the seating group, but not so large an area that the space feels empty and miserable. You shouldn't be able to walk in a straight line from one end of your room to the other. If this is the case I can almost promise you that your room will look boring as it's likely that everything is pushed against the wall. Furniture needs to float in the middle – it makes spaces far more invigorating and cosy. Instead of creating this weird dead space you actually make conversation areas more intimate and create a better sense of balance. This applies even in small spaces. Trust me, I know it sounds counterintuitive, but if you want your room to look bigger don't push everything against the walls. The 'furniture shoved against the wall' scenario is actually one of my pet peeves – it looks like a doctor's waiting room. Even in small spaces you can move the furniture away from the wall a tad so it's not physically touching. Plop a skinny shelf or console there, layer up, and 'wham bam!' magic happens, and the room actually feels bigger.

One of the best ways to get your furniture arrangement right is to experiment. Don't get stuck into one layout, move stuff around, shift, re-orientate, it will give your home a whole new lease of life! You'll need to consider focal points, conversational areas and balance. Think about both the size and placement of the pieces and make sure not all large pieces are in one area and small in the other, otherwise the room will feel off-kilter and lopsided – and therefore unsettling. Oh, and remember to introduce a variety in the shapes. If everything is straight lined, add circles. It can feel quite challenging to somehow get a room to read like it makes perfect sense. If everything is from different eras it can be hard to balance and harmonize. I love mixing, but if things get too much I cheat a little and mix in pairs. As I've mentioned before, adding a bit of symmetry makes things less chaotic. Rather than everything being different it feels more balanced. Obviously you don't want to overdo it – matching furniture sets are a major design crime!

Don't get stuck into one layout, move stuff around, shift, re-orientate, it will give your home a whole new lease of life!

I'm always trying to think of unusual combinations when it comes to mixing furniture, like putting little stools under leggy consoles or plopping a sofa next to a dining table. The Americans do this a lot – it's the ultimate luxury I reckon. For example, there is something about a plush sofa anchoring a dining table that just screams 'cool'. It's unexpected and so fabulous. Not only does it glam up the space, it adds a whole different level of comfort. Everywhere and anywhere, try to create little conversational areas to hang out in, from landings to bedrooms to living rooms. There is something so cosy about creating conversational nooks. In large rooms don't limit yourself to just one area, little intimate conversational spaces are so cosifying. In small spaces a little upholstered stool or ottoman next to an occasional chair sparks an intriguing little area. Think in layers: add benches to the end of beds; stools and chairs in bathrooms and landings; little tables everywhere. When it comes to coffee tables, more often than not I go bigger. That way they act as an anchor for the room and present a great platform to style up. It's also easier to plop seats around.

Combining old furniture with new, vintage with rustic and blending contemporary with inherited, is what makes homes truly unique. Every piece has a purpose, rooms have a sense of adventure and feel artful and full-on sensory. Once you're crossed over to the maximalist side there is no going back!

In small spaces a little upholstered stool or ottoman next to an occasional chair sparks an intriguing little area.

CREATING AMBIENCE WITH LIGHTING

The thing I love about maximalism is the opportunity it gives you to be explorative with materials in exciting new ways. Lighting is everything in this style of interiors, creating ambience, atmosphere and mood.

Often lighting gets relegated to an afterthought. We spend ages pondering over paint colours and room layouts, or the latest sofa and chairs, and put lighting on the back burner. This is a mistake, as good lighting can completely transform a space. I'm not talking about just brightening up an alcove, it's much deeper than that. Lighting affects our emotions, which directly contributes to our overall mood. I went to a restaurant not so long ago which was lit with cool LED lights and it made me feel like I was in a hospital. It was so bad I had to leave – the harsh white glare was quite frankly unbearable!

When you get the lighting right it lifts your mood, motivates you and makes you happier and far more relaxed. If you are starting from scratch or redecorating, begin by creating a lighting plan. Think about what activities take place in each room – like relaxing, sleeping, working or eating – plus any key features you want to highlight.

If you're not starting from scratch, don't worry, just think about adding multiple points of light to each and every room and make table lights your new BFF; they have transformed my interior (more on that shortly...).

Lighting can make every single room feel more charming and more attractive. Done well, it puts you under a spell. You're not even aware of it, but if it's done badly, suddenly you are super-conscious of how unflattering it can be. Like overheads that are too bright, Edison bulbs everywhere, or an isolated pendant. Lighting is actually the first impression your brain registers, before you notice anything else – cosy or austere, your brain registers it in a nanosecond.

In all my years in this business, I would say that lighting is the one area people get most wrong. It sounds so simple though, right? Plug in a lamp, flip a switch and voila! I'm afraid it's a bit more complicated than that.

All maximalist rooms need a combination of three types of lighting – overhead, accent and task – to create a layered illuminated scheme. Lighting should always and only be about layers. Unless recessed, any kind of ceiling light will make a room appear too bright. Table lamps alone will make a room appear too sombre and wall lights too dull. What we need are different light sources at different levels, as that creates ambience and interest. Up-lighting, for instance, can make rooms feel larger; low-hung pendants can create the illusion of height; clusters of lighting make rooms cosy and more intimate: so mix away!

Also think about mixing in styles, shapes, tones and textures that complement the overall design of the space but also provide contrast. Visual impact is super important with lighting. If you are mixing a lot of different styles – like in my place for instance, where I've got clay tribal lamps hanging out with little vintage French sconces, a 1950s Italian table lamp with some pieces I've brought off the high street – thread and link and harmonize them all together through colour. Not necessarily the same colour, but the same colour family (for me that is neutrals and blacks), so they seamlessly blend and look like they were meant to be together. Chandeliers, sconces, table lamps and floor lamps all come together, harmonious yet interesting.

What we need are different light sources at different levels, as that creates ambience and interest.

Never eliminate shadows, they too are so important in a space. Shadows create mystery and mystery creates intrigue. Without darker, quieter areas everything is flat and boring so we need to create this subtle interplay between light and dark. Shadows add depth, they add dimension, perspective and realism and they make corners blur and fuzz out.

Dimmers are also fundamental to any lighting scheme and, as maximalist spaces layer lighting more beautifully than any other decorative scheme I know, they are an important tool in creating atmosphere. Anything in the ceiling should be dimmable as this will add an extra dimension, taking you from maximum brightness to a softer mood setting altogether. It will give you much more flexibility as day gently moves to night, or summer shifts into autumn. By lowering the intensity of the output you create such a beautiful atmospheric, soft, ambient glow.

Which Bulb?

I am old-school: I love traditional incandescent bulbs and the warmer light they emit, but as they are no longer available, I have to get with the LED, low-energy programme.

Not all white lights are created equal, some are warm – like candlelight – and some cool – like winter. Colour temperature is measured in degrees Kelvin (K). I opt for warm coloured bulbs and go with 2000–3000K which is the warmest. The higher you go in the colour temperature range, the more blue is introduced. That blue gives an awful hospital look, which is where those bulbs should remain!

For bathrooms, bedrooms, dining and living rooms, warm white at 2000–3000K is what I suggest. For lighting specific tasks, it could be argued that cooler white bulbs (3000–4000K) are better. LED lighting is improving, it's just not quite there yet. It doesn't have the warmth of that amber glow from incandescent bulbs.

THE LIVING ROOM

I love lighting living rooms, maybe that's because they host a broad range of activities, so have quite complex needs. These multi-use spaces where we read, entertain, hang out, work and relax need a truly layered scheme. Get the lighting right and it will look magical.

Figure out where you need your task lights first, so always around your furniture arrangements. This is a focused light, and for this you will need down-lights, desk and reading lamps.

Then move onto ambient light. Ambient lighting mimics natural daylight and creates atmosphere, so think pendants, wall lamps and table lamps, to create soft, soft pools.

Accent lighting should then highlight any design features. Artworks, for example, can be highlighted with up-lights, down-lights and spots, but I mostly do it with table lamps, which create lovely soft pools of light. Introducing lighting into shelving adds further interest and depth and you could even add more drama and depth to shelves by back-lighting – this will silhouette objects beautifully.

Finally, I think all living rooms need a pendant or chandelier, a decorative fixture in the centre of the room. It's like adding that final piece of jewellery and is such a major finishing touch. Having a chandelier in the room embellishes it and makes it feel grander, cooler and more luxurious. Oh and anywhere there is a seat, add a lamp. I like to overdose on table lamps – the warm localized glow that they emit really draws the eye.

A variety of lights, from floor to table, ceiling to wall, will make any living room feel super cosy. Remember, different heights are key.

Having a chandelier in the room embellishes it and makes it feel grander, cooler and more luxurious.

WHEN YOU GET THE LIGHTING
RIGHT IT LIFTS YOUR MOOD,
MOTIVATES YOU AND MAKES
YOU HAPPIER AND FAR
MORE RELAXED.

THE KITCHEN

Lighting for kitchens is rather more complex as kitchens these days are so multi-functional. No longer just a place to whip up some roasted carrots with a smoked pesto dressing! They are increasingly places for relaxing, entertaining and even working. Get the lighting right in the kitchen and not only can it make it appear larger and cooler, it will actually make you want to linger in there longer. Obviously food prep zones – like the kitchen sink and above the hob – will require task lighting. Recessed lights in the ceiling, pendants over islands, strips of LED lights under the bottom of cabinets or shelves are all fundamental – just remember to make them dimmable. Then take these spaces to another level of coolness by adding in table and wall lights. Not only will it make your scheme feel more layered and chic, it will also create a moodier ambience that will make cooking and eating in the kitchen far more enjoyable.

THE HALLWAY

Lighting for hallways is key. It sets the first impression for visitors entering a space, so needs to be spot on. These are challenging areas to light – they are often not very big and don't have much in them – so your lighting scheme has to work doubly hard to create atmosphere and drama. Go for some sort of decorative pendant that sets the visual tone, but you will also need wall lights. Wall lamps are fabulous for narrow spaces, as are table lamps on the skinniest console or table. Remember, the more layers of light the more interest!

Lighting can make every single room feel more charming and more attractive.

THE BEDROOM

Lighting for bedrooms should be similar to living spaces and virtually every other room – this means finding the right balance between ambient, task and accent. Begin with the foundation: ambient lighting. Ceiling fixtures like chandeliers and pendants are a good place to start, and then floor lamps. On top of this general light, layer in task lighting for activities that require a bit more focus like reading and even working – consider table lights, low-hanging pendants, sconces, and wall-mounted task lights. Accent lighting in the bedroom acts as a subdued version of ambient, creating a cosy atmosphere and giving off a pleasant glow. Table lamps and walls sconces are great for this. Again I would always go for a central chandelier, have two bedside lamps for reading (not the same style mind), with table lamps scattered throughout on consoles and dressers and then finish off with the odd floor lamp in a corner.

Shadows add depth, they add dimension, perspective and realism and they make corners blur and fuzz out.

THE BATHROOM

Bathrooms need four types of lighting: task, ambient, decorative, oh and a little sparkle! Task lighting around the mirror is key. A pair of sconces mounted at eye level on either side of the mirror means you get no shadows and it's the best scenario for shaving, applying make up and so on.

Putting art or sculpture in a bathroom takes it to another level and accent lighting will show it off the best. Decorative lighting adds a further dimension of interest so a beautiful pendant or chandelier over the bath will do the trick.

Ambient lighting of course cannot be neglected – anything recessed or any pendants with translucent shades will do the trick, all on dimmers, of course! I always want to create a sense of intimacy in the bathroom so it feels spa-like and luxurious. Add a cluster of candles and the odd decorative table lamp and you're there.

FIXTURES AND LAMPS

Choosing the right fixture can completely transform a dull, boring space into a cosy, inviting retreat. Beyond being a commodity, think of a lamp as a piece that actually changes up a room's atmosphere. In terms of styles, the choices are endless – from rustic to traditional, contemporary to glam. I tend to lean towards lights that enhance my existing decor and complement it rather than standing out, but there is no right or no wrong.

There are so many options out there, but table lamps are the ones that I find the most transformative. They are less fancy that decorative chandeliers and tall floor lamps and are my go-to tools for changing up the mood. You can use them to add colour, contrast or texture and to introduce symmetry should you want. With a style of their own they can exclusively sit within the style of a room or at the very same time usher in a completely different vibe, giving the space a whole new interesting focal point. The choices out there are numerous. From industrial to sparkling gold, you can bring in any hue of your choice. Add a punch, don't add a punch. Dial the mood up, dial the mood down. You can blend in seamlessly, or you can stand out. Something I do time and time again is to mix two completely different table lamps with similar colours or geometric shapes together to give the room more visual symmetry.

The same goes for pendants – they really define a room. Positioned alone over a bath tub, or clustered together over a central kitchen island, they define a space and can turn a dull room into a dramatic one. There are three uses for pendant lights: ambient, task lighting or accent lighting (which highlights specific areas). When you are choosing pendants for overall lighting consider a pendant with a light diffuser or use semi-opaque bulbs. With task lighting choose pendants that are open at the top. This ensures the light underneath is not too harsh. For feature and accent lighting, always add a dimmer. Fabric light fixtures cast a softer glow, as the light is diffused through the fabric shade. For task lighting, glass or acrylic maximizes the light output.

I tend to lean towards lights that enhance my existing decor and complement it rather than standing out, but there is no right or no wrong.

Floor lamps add instant height to a room. This really helps in a maximalist space, as we want constantly to take the eye up, as that makes rooms feel grander. A classic interior design trick is to use verticals to make the space feel bigger. Tall, skinny floor lamps do just that, not forgetting how much colour, texture and character they can add. They are great for empty corners and so easily transform a room. No need for a complete overhaul – I use floor lamps like a secret weapon! They can be used for all three kinds of lighting (ambient, task and accent) and they can do this separately or simultaneously. For example, have a few dotted around a living room to create ambient light, position near a chair for task and place near a painting to highlight (or accent)! Their lovely pools of light can create a new mood and they really upgrade a scheme. Whether they complement, or stand out and clash they bring so much to the table!

I am the hugest fan of wall lights – they make spaces feel cosier, cooler and more balanced by diffusing and contouring light. They can direct light up or down. Up-lights direct light towards the ceiling so they draw attention and are great for making a room appear larger than it really is. Down-lights allow light at the bottom, so the higher you place the fixture the more the light will be cast down. I love down-lights, they are great for creating a warm, cosy glow. Both are fundamental in layered maximalist lighting schemes. When you have light shining through the top and bottom, your scheme will feel more balanced as the light is distributed more evenly. In bathrooms wall lights are great flanking a mirror, adding visual balance.

In kitchens a layered lighting approach (often overlooked although it is so important) with wall lights either side of a cooker, say, or on a wall where food prep takes place, or over the sink, will add so much visual interest. In bedrooms, adding wall lights either side of the bed is beautiful and in living rooms you can go just above eye level to avoid any glare. Also consider having some lower down, so that they become reading lights that can be angled to illuminate the pages of a book. In hallways they are perhaps needed the most, adding visual interest to awkward narrow areas – they are something to walk towards. They can provide helpful little pops of light that can also highlight artworks, or architectural elements, where you can angle the shade to throw light upwards, nice! I like nothing better than putting wall lights on the outside of my bookcases. It makes my display of books and endless interiors magazines more of a feature. Even when they are not switched on they create an interesting sculptural aesthetic.

A classic interior design trick is to use verticals to make the space feel bigger. Tall, skinny floor lamps do just that, not forgetting how much colour, texture and character they can add.

No matter how big or small your space, whether you live on the coast or in the country, uptown or downtown, adding a little extra dose of sparkle goes a long way. If I'm ever in a lighting conundrum, I find adding a string of fairy lights adds instant glamour, elevating my space in a matter of seconds, creating atmosphere and making the most of a special feature. Draped around mirrors, fireplaces, on wreaths (I do this a lot) and as centrepieces, they create a magical glow. Use them to give shelves a little 'je ne sais quoi', drape over plants and even take them outside. I've layered them over artworks, giving my walls texture, or draped around the edges of cabinets. The string of twinkly lights draws attention to my displays. No longer just reserved for the Christmas tree they make any space completely magical. I use them all year round as they add such sparkle.

SIZE AND SCALE

Let's talk scale for a moment. I would encourage you to supersize the odd lamp in each room. You only need to do it once, and it creates such a grand gesture. Whether it's a chandelier, pendant or table lamp, it adds such a magical flourish. An oversized pendant over a bathtub, or a cluster of pendants over a staircase, it's a clever trick to use something that instinctively feels too large. It creates visual interest and adds an important focal point for styling other elements like plants, books or candles. In my mind, bigger is always better, as it makes such a decorative statement. I love a dramatic fixture in hallways, or over dining tables, but remember when you go big on the odd fixture everything else needs to be smaller in scale so as not to compete.

HOW MANY LAMPS?

More is more when it comes to numbers in a maximalist's space. The average room needs around 8–10 lamps. The advantage in having lots of different light sources is that you will have far more flexibility with choosing which elements of the room you want to highlight and draw the eye to, plus you will get all these pockets of beautiful glow.

FINISHES

Materials and finishes are also extremely important when it comes to lighting. In darker spaces I like to go a little blingy with reflective materials, like brass, crystal and glass. This enhances brightness, but don't go overboard. As with everything, variety is key. Matchy-matchy works for wall sconces that flank a mirror or a bed or even a couple of pendants over a kitchen island, but you wouldn't want your table and floor lamps to match – that's way too dull.

Don't forget about the surfaces that the lamps will sit on. Wood, for example, is warmer to bounce light off than, say, stainless steel or glass. Place a lamp in front of a mirror and magic happens: you will double the light in a room. Mirrored surfaces are great for bouncing light around. Gloss paint does the same thing, as do glass and marble.

LIGHTING ERRORS

If a room is lit well, everything looks at its best and feels relaxed and comfortable. If your space feels a little off, take a step back and see if you have made one of these lighting blunders.

→ One of the most common mistakes is the reliance on the overhead light or rather an abundance of overhead lights, such as recessed lights. The light that overheads cast is dull so they should never be on their own. They need their buddies, task and decorative lights, to be on at the same time, otherwise the space will never feel cosy and atmospheric. You can't create that intimacy that maximalist interiors so crave with recessed lights and overheads alone – always think in layers. If the lighting feels wrong, ask yourself – do you have enough accent lights?

→ Often the floor and not the walls are being lit. Let's say you've got the pendant over the table, or spotlights in the hallway, it's not actually going to be enough. You are lighting the floor with overhead lights. Highlight the walls as well – if you have any spots close to the perimeter of your rooms angle lamps towards the walls. This provides a wash of light that is reflected back into the room – beautiful, especially if your walls happen to have a texture like a grasscloth wallpaper or exposed brick. It's a much softer scheme and when you light the walls your eye is instantly drawn to the edges, creating the illusion of more space.

→ It is easy to neglect low-level lighting. Pop a few up-lighters at floor level and you can cast the most beautiful shadows. Hotels are particularly good at doing this. You can highlight a fireplace, a freestanding bath or the base of a large plant. Add LEDs to kickboards for an additional atmospheric glow! Ideally you'll want more than one circuit to allow you to create different scenes and moods at different times of day – this is super important.

More is more when it comes to numbers in a maximalist's space. The average room needs around 8–10 lamps.

Don't forget the outside space. Any rooms that look onto gardens or balconies should connect in terms of colour palettes and materiality. If you want to draw attention to a specimen tree, border or trug, consider some well-placed uplights and some white accessories, from furnishings to pots. This will bounce the light around and help extend the perceived size of the area.

Look at lighting your maximalist space like one of those Instagram feeds we are all so drawn to following. The swoon-worthy, snug sanctuaries that look like they belong in a Dutch Master's painting or a Tom Ford film. Fabrics shimmer and fold under the light, materials are softly lit. The lighting feels sensitive and sensual. Mastering this is like being an alchemist. It feels magical.

STYLING YOUR SPACE

You can make any room into one that awakens all the senses and is truly show-stopping through storytelling. How? By layering and styling your accessories, textiles, colour and furnishings to create personally meaningful interiors.

By using my tried and tested techniques, you'll soon be styling like a pro to produce interiors that feel curated, collected and cool. Spaces that evoke a sense of warmth and relaxation. Like most things, it all comes down to the details. Don't worry about how eclectic your accessories may be, the trick is being able to pull them all together so they feel natural, individual and as if they were always meant to hang together. Layering is my secret weapon in making rooms feel extraordinary. Everything comes down to this one special word, 'vignette': a technique that you apply to objects to make them feel appealing. When you put your vignette hat on you have the power to transform absolutely everything!

CREATING A VIGNETTE

In the world of interior design, a vignette is a grouping of things, or an arrangement that creates an interesting focal point. Pieces look balanced and the objects tell a story about you and your home. By melding a variety of objects together in an artistic way you can create the most harmonious tableaux. Things haven't just been plonked, they have been curated.

There are tricks to pulling off vignettes (aren't there always?) and you can create them anywhere from mantles, to coffee tables, sideboards, end tables or entry tables. In fact wherever there is a surface always think of creating a vignette: a small scene that looks effortlessly composed and eye-catching. So, how to go about it?

→ You first need to choose a hero item, one that your eye will immediately zoom to and the first place it naturally rests upon. I'm talking about a statement piece – something swoon-worthy with enough visual weight and height to make a real impact. You don't want too many hero items in the same place as they will fight against each other and end up looking messy. If it's a small piece it will be swamped by other objects in the grouping so start big. Something like a piece of sculpture, a tall vase of flowers, a painting, a lamp or a mirror – something to give your composition some height.

→ Then cluster in some other items – let's say books, candles, artworks and smaller photos – and place these around the larger hero piece.

→ To give your vignette more cohesion superimpose an imaginary 'A' shape or triangle over the grouping. This is a trick you can use time and time again, especially if you are new to styling, as it will prevent your vignette having a long skyline effect which tends to scatter the focus. Position the shorter objects towards the outer edges, with taller ones in the centre, and voila – you have your 'A' shape.

→ For anything more linear, let's say a long sideboard, a console or a shelf, ditch the 'A' rule and instead make sure there is a strong relationship between all the pieces in the arrangement. One or two pieces need to be supersized, so again think tall – art pieces, mirrors and lamps are all great for this. Rather than leave large gaps between objects, play around with the heights and cross things over, intersect and butt them up. Link them together through colour, texture, pattern and material but also contrast some pieces to make things interesting.

→ If you want to create unstudied loose gatherings where the eye moves around at ease, introduce asymmetry to your vignettes. Asymmetry is the most interesting type of balance and is rather key to maximalist spaces. Many interiors don't feel artfully layered and that is because they are too symmetrical. If you mix rather than double up objects it shakes things up. For example, a console asymmetrically designed might feature a mirror down one end, and a painting down the other, both of similar visual weight. In the middle: a sculpture, photos, candles, decorative boxes. You still need to make it feel balanced so repeat form, material, colour and lines but without mirroring or exact duplication. Maximalist spaces embrace asymmetrical vignettes so rooms feel automatically more lived in, loved and casual. Oh, and asymmetry isn't only about going big with huge statement works of art, you can make the biggest statement by pivoting a cluster of books with a candle on top on an angle.

Joshua Yeldham   SURRENDER

ay   Amber Creswell Bell

loose leaf

MICKEY
ROBERTSON   The HOUSE and GARDEN
at GLENMORE

Living in the Countryside   TASCHEN

MARTYN THOMPSON
WORKING SPACE

MAISON CHRISTIAN LIAIGRE

RALPH LAUREN

197

IN THE WORLD OF INTERIOR
DESIGN, A VIGNETTE IS A
GROUPING OF THINGS, OR
AN ARRANGEMENT THAT
CREATES AN INTERESTING
FOCAL POINT.

→ When it comes to styling, balance is key.
  We need things to look appealing and cohesive.
  You wouldn't place a large mirror down at one
  end of a console and at the other end have a
  small plant, for instance. That would feel too
  lopsided. Instead, balance the mirror with a
  taller lamp or painting. That way it will visually
  connect; the weights will read as similar.
  Having said that, we always need a varied
  landscape so when placing objects together
  imagine a cityscape where there is a mix of
  heights rather than a strict line-up. Short,
  medium and tall items keep the eye darting
  around and interested.

→ Your background will have a significant impact
  on your vignette; highly patterned wallpapers
  with a colourful artwork in front can cause
  visual chaos so always consider the background
  when layering up. The colour and/or pattern
  on the wall behind will form the basis for
  your vignette and will really dominate the
  composition, so tread carefully.

→ Equally important is the surface under your
  vignette. If your sideboard happens to be
  elaborately carved with an elegant wood grain
  or marquetry it will distract from the grouping,
  so in cases like that don't overload the display.
  Let the surface shine. Anything simple and
  clean-cut can, of course, have far more on it.

→ The easiest way to make maximalist spaces feel curated is to give the items in your grouping a reason to hang together. By repeating colours, textures, materials, shapes and even pattern, the eye will travel enjoyably around your vignette.

→ We also need friction (see pages 52–56) and contrast – unexpected juxtapositions that enliven the eye. An old antique vase that has a beautiful patina combined with textural mossy foliage brought in from the garden, for instance, would look beautiful. Perhaps a smooth glossy succulent in a roughly woven basket. Contrast is key – it keeps things interesting and intriguing.

→ Connection is key. If you don't intersect and cross over your objects they lose their bond and may look like they are set out for a garage sale! Constantly think about visually linking everything. Hang a mirror, or artwork a little too low so objects encroach on it.

→ Step back from your assembled vignette and examine it in detail. Does it need more or less? I am forever editing and pulling things back.

WHAT TO USE IN A VIGNETTE?

Books are my number one go-to accessory as they give vignettes such depth, pattern, colour and intrigue. They are such representations of our passions and interests. You can stack them to varying heights and they can hold smaller objects like candles and plants to feel more layered. Books instantly make a space feel homely. Stack both vertically and horizontally to keeps things interesting. Upright books feel more poised and horizontal books can serve as pedestals for accessories. With anything too shiny, I whip off the jacket and usually reveal something more matt and rustic underneath.

If you have a lot of small accessories of similar heights, anchor them on a tray or platter. This will make your arrangement feel more stylized and is a must for uniting random objects. Oh, and always think about heights, even on low surfaces like coffee tables. Stack books, add in boxes, it all brings interest.

Pitchers, ceramic vases, bowls – these are all pieces that have a real presence and lend visual oomph.

You can cluster plants for impact, and play around with shapes and finishes: feathery, shiny, pointy, glossy, matt.

It is easy to come undone when you begin styling shelves and tables but a simple trick is to always start with the larger items first, whether those are woven baskets, artworks, or sculptures. This will help you get the scale and balance right as well as giving you your basic layout. The minute you take your vignette up a level is when you introduce decorative objects. Any pieces you've collected from your travels will work really well, some of my most loved pieces are items I've found in markets or souks in Asia or the Middle East. An old tureen that I cook in almost every day sits so beautifully on my shelf, as does a hand-hammered metal bowl from India. Pitchers, ceramic vases, bowls – these are all pieces that have a real presence and lend visual oomph. Plus they are good anchoring pieces.

Clear accessories are fab for maximalist spaces – anything like glass bowls or acrylic boxes – adding layers without blocking what is behind them. Items that catch the light – like tea lights, mirrored boxes, gilded frames and bowls – add a whole other dimension. Shiny and clear surfaces break up dense arrangements so they don't feel too heavy.

Nothing brings a room or an arrangement to life like flowers and plants. When in doubt (even when not in doubt!), add in some botanicals. This is the simplest and easiest way to add extra and instant dimension. I use flowers and plants like I would an accessory. They enliven nooks, from single stems to little clusters of cacti, and are a powerful tool in my decorating arsenal. You can group plants for impact, and play around with shapes and finishes: feathery, shiny, pointy, glossy, matt. Just keep pots similar in hue to elevate the botanical even further. Restrict the colours and up the texture.

Always, always, always introduce curves in your tableaux. Curves break up straight lines in arrangements and rooms – they have a miraculous ability to remove edges from your line of sight, making rooms appear softer. Curves give us a sense of comfort and security. A curved vase, ornamental pot or candle softens the harder edges found on mirrors and paintings and serves as a counterpoint. When you add round objects to linear furniture or shelves the strong horizontal lines of the piece are balanced beautifully by the curvier pieces. Curves pull the eye around.

Maximalist spaces typically feel invigorating as well as relaxed and one of the tricks to achieving that is the balance of open storage with closed storage. So anything utilitarian goes away out of sight and into drawers and then more decorative, beautiful pieces like vases, candleholders or coffee table books come to the fore on open shelves and surfaces. When you edit like this you are actually making your objects look and feel more important, rather than just having a lot of stuff out. Grouping collections like bowls, masks, or pottery makes any arrangement feel more considered and luxurious than having things all over the house. You are creating settings that your eye can rest upon.

Groupings of artworks are an amazing way to infuse colour, texture and pattern into your maximalist space. Don't be afraid to mix different periods and styles – from kids' art to works painted on canvas to posters and flea market finds. I personally think walls hung with photos, paintings and prints set such an expressive vibe and are an excellent way of injecting personality.

Forget hanging for a moment and consider leaning art against a wall, on a table or on the floor, it can be super casual and cool. Cluster a bunch together of varying heights but similar moods into your vignette so that it feels considered and as if it belongs. That could be on a console or the floor – it adds so much dimension. When you vary the display everything looks more interesting as you are using different techniques so hang, prop, stack or lean.

PLACES FOR VIGNETTES

Shelves have the ability to completely turn rooms around, whether they are floating (ones that appear to levitate with their hidden brackets), built-in or freestanding. They are great places to show off collections and elevate your pieces. You can go floor hugging with a piece that spans the room or choose skeletal shelves in a dining room, for example, that instil more order.

When you edit like this you are actually making your objects look and feel more important, rather than just having a lot of stuff out.

Vignettes are a great vehicle for drawing the eye away from anything problematic and they are so easy to pull off. Tricky alcoves can be transformed with a few simple shelves, a stack of books, some art, the odd botanical, a lamp and possibly a stool at the base. I love to paint shelves the same colour as the wall so my accessories headline the show and the shelf itself seems to disappear. Establishing a palette will make the shelves feel more pulled together.

Use points of light everywhere, from a wall light highlighting an artwork to mini table lamps on sideboards and shelves to add gravitas. Shelves always need to feel bountiful, loaded and well stocked, so pile things up and remember to vary tones, textures and colours. If it's all beginning to look too much introduce white accents, as white calms the mind. Think of adding in white flowers, like hydrangeas, milky handthrown ceramics or a cream-coloured lamp.

The thing about layers, and layering your vignettes, is that they increase your physical comfort by pleasing the eye. I know there is a fine line between randomly grouping pieces to full-on clutter but that is what vignettes add to our maximalist spaces. They make that unique combination of objects feel effortless. Haphazard arrangements can feel collected if you layer your arrangements in groupings. Groupings attract attention and create strong focal points. Remember always to vary heights and widths, I know it sounds obvious but too many pieces that are spindly or, conversely, bulky, won't make for an interesting scheme.

Don't just stop there, layer up rugs, bring large plants into the mix and overlap everything. When you partially obscure something you create a sense of mystery. Something like a lamp overlapping a piece of art, for instance, or a vase overlapping a sculpture. It makes you want to explore the space more and makes interiors far more compelling.

If you're in a conundrum about where to start with a vignette, bar carts are excellent mobile tables that will make any alcove or nook feel special. I always include something unexpected like a sculpture, a piece of framed art (leaning or hung) and a lamp. Edit down the booze and just add the odd pretty decanter, a cactus, and stack of books – sorted!

Mantles are obvious places for vignettes; I like to anchor with a mirror or large piece of art which more or less dictates the rest of the scheme. Aim for a mix of heights and colours to keep the eye moving, and remember the books and botanicals.

Dressers are great for layering up. Work from the tallest accessory out – leaning, propping, intersecting. Art always works; then try adding a lamp, a pretty dish, a vase of flowers and a candle on top of some books. Remember to include a mix of textures (shiny, matt, rough and smooth) and also juggle around the heights to create an interesting landscape.

Groupings attract attention and create strong focal points. And they give the space just the right dose of the unexpected.

Learn to trust your eye and break a few rules.

When it comes to styling coffee tables, always look down at them from above. Choose items that mimic the shape of the table, from boxes to books, and then add in the odd circular piece (if the table happens to be square or rectangular) to break everything up. Stacks of things are good as they add depth to a horizontal plane. Oh, and always include a box to hide ugly remotes!

A smidge of humour, something unexpected or a little bit quirky makes rooms feel more liveable and humanizes them. Rooms that feel overly decorated can feel self-important and static. Loose, easy-going and comfortable is where they should be at. Always add in the odd irreverent accent like some whimsical touches that don't take themselves too seriously, from a ceramic poodle lamp to a little Easter Island sculpture. One of the easiest decorating tricks around is adding pieces that make your heart skip a beat. They require no skill or complex understanding of anything other than what makes you smile. They imperceptibly lift your mood – they are

happy pieces – and can be anything like animals, sculptures or kids' art. Learn to trust your eye and break a few rules. Hang pictures just below eye level and anchor with a little stool or table, a heap of books and a lamp. Lovely!

Simply collecting stuff is not enough. I read somewhere that objects are like words, they need to be made into meaningful sentences. Little nothings like notes, postcards or matchboxes can look beautiful when threaded into art, placed near vases and thoughtfully clustered. Styling is about groupings that create strong visual statements.

No matter what you mix, insignificant or significant, when pieces share a colour, material, tone or shape they instantly and always make a worthy vignette.

I think one of my absolute pleasures in life is to rearrange and re-layer things, pictures, books, smaller possessions – it's so much fun. Vignettes don't just happen, they are tweaked, edited, thought about and considered. When you get that dialogue right, magic happens.

CHALLENGE THE NORM

Two vital elements – pattern and texture – should never be underestimated in maximalist spaces. You can create the most compelling interiors by playing with an incredible melting pot of materials and motifs. Each element can vibrate with energy or it can calm, restore and soothe. Getting the pattern right and the texture on point will help you to create beautiful spaces.

Both pattern and texture have the ability to tell a story, a narrative about you. Want a cosy, boho vibe? Then rough absorbing textures provide that feeling of warmth. Tribal, loose, free-flowing patterns give it a laid-back vibe. From bold stripes to plaids, ikats to deeply hued geometrics, softly woven blankets, to lime wash, honed marble to cerused wood, lacquered brass to poured concrete, these elements – when partnered correctly – can make homes appear more balanced, welcoming and way cooler than you could ever have imagined.

No space is complete without the interplay between texture and pattern. You might have the right lighting, the most incredible colour scheme, a beautiful array of accessories even, but unless you understand how to combine, play up and dial down these two major elements you won't be able to take your rooms to the next level. I think of pattern and texture like herbs or spices – they add pizzazz and depth.

TEXTURE

Have you ever decorated a room and wondered what's missing? Can't quite put your finger on it? More than likely, texture is the elusive component. Texture creates comfort, interest and focal points – it's super clever. I find that it is so often overlooked, which sounds rather odd as everything has its own texture, right? True, but it's working with the right textures that is fundamental for maximalist spaces.

There are two ways to read texture:

→ In a visual way: it immediately appeals to your visual sense at first glance.

→ In a tactile way: it almost compels you to stroke it by igniting your sense of touch.

A clever combination of the two is what adds real depth to a space.

As with everything maximalist, it's all in the mix. Think about partnering smooth, silky, glossy, with rough, natural and slubby. When you mix textures you excite the mind by creating movement, intrigue and depth. Smooth, rough, bumpy or flat, the surface quality of a material will have a big impact on your space. More interestingly, when you actually look at the surface of a material your perception of that surface is greatly influenced by the adjacent texture, which is why, in this instance, you want them to be opposing. So when you partner rough surfaces next to smooth ones you are actually elevating both of them. Rough surfaces seem more textured, and smooth surfaces seem even smoother and flatter. Clever, no?

Playing with texture means working with all sorts of surfaces, from uneven to reflective, and it's the interplay of light and shadow on those surfaces that creates so much intrigue. The way the light interacts with the texture will add all sorts of character, dimension and depth, not to mention atmosphere.

Certain textures absorb or diffuse light and others reflect it. Silk, satin, stainless steel, glossy paint and marble all possess lustrous qualities that reflect light and therefore brighten a space. Rough stone, weathered wood and linen do the opposite and absorb light so the impact of their colour is subtler and these textures feel warmer and softer. So if you want to introduce more light into a space use reflective materials, and use darker more absorbent materials when the level of light is too much or you need to make it feel cosier and more snug.

True magic happens when you partner, say, a luxuriously upholstered velvet armchair with a silk cushion, next to a luminous glass lamp with a raffia shade which casts pools of soft glowing light onto a woollen rug. Glossy reflective textures with more absorbent materials – super nice! Wool is actually an opaque fibre that neither refracts or reflects light, but it's such a grounding, cosy material I actually use it everywhere!

Different textures have a major impact on mood and so to create your dream maximalist space you need to consider each texture individually but then also as a whole, layering and combining them with others to create depth and visual intrigue throughout. Remember also that texture comes from the room itself, it's not just about what you fill it with. Walls, floors and ceilings (our largest surface areas) all contribute and can be given the most wondrous textural

When you mix textures you excite the mind by creating movement, intrigue and depth. Smooth, rough, bumpy or flat, the surface quality of a material will have a big impact on your space.

treatments, from the most beautiful lime wash paint to glossy tiles; smoothly poured concrete floors to roughly hewn wooden ones.

Repeat, repeat, repeat the textures in your room. Otherwise rooms can feel overloaded and off balance. If I were to list what's on my own 'textural spectrum' I know that I instinctively lean towards more slubby, cocooning textures as opposed to glossy, shiny ones. It's personal, obviously, but those textures are comforting and that's how I want to feel in my room, wrapped up in a snug textural blanket. However, I still need to pepper in glossier, smoother surfaces, or it would feel too much. It's a balancing act, so trust your intuition. If your home doesn't feel cosy enough introduce slubbier textures, if it feels too much pare it back and introduce some more reflective pieces.

The best thing about texture is that you can never really overdo it. Unlike pattern, where you have to continually pull back to avoid things looking chaotic, you have far greater flexibility with texture. There are lots of easy ways to bring texture into your space.

→ The quickest way to up the textural levels in a space is through textiles: cushions, bedding, throws and rugs. I call these items the 'five-minute face-lifters' of the decorating world. They can change the feel of a space in minutes. I happen to think that rugs complete a room, making it feel more welcoming. I have them everywhere, from landings to hallways, bathrooms to bedrooms. You can layer multiple rugs over each other, mix flat weaves with slubby, kilims with Berber, there are so many incredible choices.

→ Botanicals add oodles of texture. I love feathery pampas grass in, say, a sculptural vase or seedpods in a roughly thrown clay vessel. Withering branches, boughs laden with moss, a long stem of eucalyptus – different shapes, different hues of green and brown all hang out together. I dial down the colour and ramp up the texture to keep things interesting, so rather than the colour being the star, the texture is. Not only is there a difference in form, leaf shape, petal, hue and height, there is also a difference in the dull, matt, shiny and glossy textures, producing the most compelling effect. Each botanical plays up and down the saturation level of green and brown but then I link them even further. I'll position feathery pampas grass against my matt painted walls, place matt trailing foliage on my smooth stone central island and add shiny eucalyptus stems near a handwoven basket. Shiny, satin, matt, dull, slubby – beautiful combinations. Everything links, everything is different.

And anyone who knows me will know how obsessed I am with faux botanicals, in fact I've made it my mission to make them chic again. The best ones are hand painted with beautiful faded colours, making them look super realistic. They are so easy to style, add lots of texture to your home and you get to keep them forever!

The coolest spaces embracing the maximalist vibe display definite consciousness in their textural decisions and therefore spaces feel more compelling, more unexpected and more intriguing.

→ Furniture finishes play an important role texturally and – considering these pieces are often large – will have a big impact on how your home feels. The texture on a piece of furniture can create a subtle focal point, like wood or metal, stone or concrete, or you can go for more of a statement. A sofa upholstered in a cashmere/mohair combo in a deep saffron yellow sets an entirely different mood. Just remember to contrast as much as you can. On leather chairs I chuck woollen cushions and sheepskins, on metal tables I place wooden pots and trailing foliage. I am forever thinking about contrasts.

→ Books are a fabulous texturizer, I have them everywhere. From little piles on side tables, shelves and coffee tables to a floor-to-ceiling bookcase in my office where I've stacked them both vertically and horizontally. Shiny covers or matt, patterned or plain, they are compelling groupings that add so much depth.

→ Think beyond the obvious when introducing texture – what about lampshades, little handthrown pots, occasional tables, wallpaper, paint? Matt glazed pots on bookcases, next to a glossy frame, or a softly woven rug butting up to a stone hearth. Everything can be thought of in terms of layers – immersive and arresting layers that are multi-dimensional and bring huge amounts of joy.

The best thing about texture is that you can never really overdo it.

227

Adding Texture with Light

Lighting plays a huge role in the texturing of a room. A handthrown ceramic table lamp feels very different from a chrome pendant, for example. Warm light produces a softer more ambient glow, white light feels harsher. Where you position lamps is key. A corner nook can blossom into the most beckoning reading area; a kitchen island can be lit up with spots a bit like a stage. It's all about mixing the styles, choosing the right bulb (see page 164) and having various levels of light throughout so you get a compelling, illuminated, textural space. For example, a light shining on a wall skimmed in lime wash or concrete casts the most incredible shadows. Directly lighting a surface will enhance it, whereas diffused lighting will detract from it and create blurred-out corners and mystery.

A word of warning... The more texture you introduce, the more you will need to restrict the colour palette, otherwise your space will read like a hot mess. You can't mix a zillion different styles and periods and textures without restricting the colour palette – otherwise rooms just won't feel considered. As much as it's great to contrast our interesting assortments, they have to be sympathetic to each other. Yes, variation is key, but they have to link in order to delight the eye.

However, rooms with only a few textures feel too one-dimensional, so don't be afraid to take some textural chances. Imagine a dining room with a smooth concrete floor, a glossy laminated table, shiny metal chairs, oh and a sleek lacquered cabinet in the corner. Everything is smooth so therefore the room feels sterile and unappealing. Texture can make or break a space, so buy what you love (that way you'll always have a place for it regardless of trends) but then make sure you think about the texture – whether it's super shiny or more subdued and absorbentor matt – and mix away.

I think there is a misconception that maximalist stylists just throw in a heap of different materials and textures and kind of hope for the best. The coolest spaces embracing the maximalist vibe display definite consciousness in the textural decisions and therefore the spaces feel more compelling, unexpected and intriguing.

PATTERN

Maximalist interiors love pattern because it adds interest and drama. Amazing things begin to happen when you play around with scale, start being ingenious with colour and mix up motifs. Rooms are given a jolt of energy and interest, not to mention contrast. Get it right and suddenly you've added depth and dimension. It's actually the simplest thing you can do to create that very overused term 'wow factor' in a room. You don't need to actually know anything about interior design to make patterns work, as there is no exact formula. All you need to do is to go with what you love and then in next to no time you will become an expert mix master!

If a room is lacking in visual weight (a kind of visual hierarchy of symmetry, balance and harmony within a space), pattern is the way to go. By adding a patterned footstool, or chair, you've suddenly upped the style ratings.

Pattern creates depth by drawing the eye, and what I love most is that it takes a two-dimensional surface and gives it an almost three-dimensional presence. This doesn't mean you have to wallpaper everywhere head-to-toe in stripes. To create intrigue you can add pattern in the simplest of ways. I know that pulling together a scheme with the perfect combo of patterns can feel a little overwhelming and a whole lot intimidating but don't be afraid. There are a few hard and fast tricks to learn if you want rooms to feel compelling and eclectic as opposed to cluttered and chaotic.

→ Start with the basics. One of the biggest challenges when mixing patterns is fear, we are all afraid of making a room look a mess. Learn to trust your eye. You need to have confidence and the simplest way to do that is to start with a colour palette. When you are working with a colour palette you love, you will automatically create consistency between your patterns, so nail that first. Decide upon your hues – warm or cool, dark or light – and rein in the number of colours you are going to use. This will keep things more cohesive and make mixing patterns that much easier.

→ Consider going for a solid background colour on some of your patterned pieces. This creates visual interest without being too taxing. Having a neutral as a background is one of the easiest ways to mix pattern and if you're new to pattern mixology it's a good way to start. It creates a statement without feeling overabundant. You don't want too many patterns on top of each other as the eye needs a place to rest. Solids balance and separate and make everything look and feel cooler and more considered.

→ Repeating patterns will make things feel less disparate. I tend to choose an overall pattern that I am quite drawn to, in my case tribal prints, and build from there. I then repeat the print (not the same motif just the same vibe throughout) in cushions, in pots and in rugs. Or say you have a stripe in your artwork; repeat that in a cushion, on a rug, in a plate.

→ You don't want zillions of patterns fighting for attention in a room because it will be chaotic, so break them up with solids. Here I'm talking about solids used in sofa upholstery or wall paint, for example. Patterns actually need solids in order to feel engaging and not messy.

→ In order for any room to feel balanced you need at least three patterns. This will give you an even distribution of pattern throughout so things feel equalized. In fact, I often tend to have more than three, and the simplest way to do this is to pick colours that harmonize as opposed to fight. Reds, pinks and caramels are my favourite base colours with a bit of black threaded through for punch. It's the simplest way to pull a room together. Use prints in similar tones and then you can pop them everywhere. It's a personal thing, obviously, but I steer clear of mixing jewel tones with pastels, or primary hues with muted colours, but go with what you love.

Maximalist interiors love pattern because it adds interest and drama.

→ When it comes to mixing, think 'opposites attract'! Offset structural prints such as grid patterns with sinuous loose prints like florals. Juxtapose a tiny print alongside an exaggerated print – it's eye-catching and dynamic. Just remember to connect them somehow (staying within the same colour family is the easiest way to that). Don't get too hung up about pattern size, just go with how you feel instinctively. Larger prints, like geometrics, can feel decorative and a lot of small pattern can feel too busy. I tend to use smaller patterns and motifs in smaller pieces like cushions and vases and reserve larger motifs for wallpaper, pendants or even art. You do need to have both – a room with only strong patterns in it will feel overpowering, so it needs its more subdued buddies to dial it down. The more variety of scale, the more intriguing and welcoming your home will feel. Some of my favourite combos are paisleys with graphics, ikats with tribals, animal print with anything from polka dots to florals, and not forgetting toile with stripes.

→ Don't get too hung up about primary, secondary and accent patterns. Many designers follow the 60/30/10 rule, where 60 per cent of a room gets one pattern (the primary), 30 per cent another (the secondary) and 10 per cent the accent pattern. The theory goes that by selecting the largest pattern first it acts as a kind of jumping off point for everything else. By all means follow that principle if you are new to pattern and you find it helpful, but I prefer to decorate a little more instinctively.

→ Don't be scared of bold colours in your prints. Deep winey burgundies or midnight blues, there is such a wide range of incredible colours to choose from. If your patterns happen to embrace these 'linger longer' colours, hats off – they are exciting and invigorating.

→ Remember to layer your patterns rather than having them all scattered all over the place and try to group them in odd numbers. Odd numbers are more pleasing to the eye and layering adds so much depth. When you place a print lampshade near a print cushion with a patterned rug below, magic happens.

→ Vertical designs like stripes will give the impression of more height, drawing the eye up. Horizontal patterns will shorten the length of the room but they will draw the eye across, increasing the width of the space, and hence make it feel wider. Conversely, round patterns can make a room appear softer and create a feeling of more space. Patterns are clever!

PUT PATTERN ON REPEAT.
ONE PATTERNED CUSHION
ALONE WILL SEEM
INSIGNIFICANT, BUT
WHEN YOU REPEAT IT
OVER AND OVER YOU GET
MOVEMENT, ENERGY AND
A SENSE OF EXCITEMENT.

CHUCK CLOSE
PRINTS, PROCESS AND COLLABORATION

Museum of
Contemporary
Art

Nothing livens up a room quite like pattern; and there are so many options out there. To get you started, and from a low-level risk point of view, try clustering some patterned cushions on a solidly upholstered sofa or chair. This will help give the room immediate dimension. A beautiful print on a wall takes things to a whole new level, adding all the liveliness you need. Go more adventurous still and pop a patterned cushion on a patterned chair. Nice! Any kind of rug that is patterned scores big points in my world, adding a punch to the space and transforming boring rooms. In fact, I would say that all rugs should have some motif or pattern on them, this is one of the quickest ways to transform a room. If you're feeling brave, you can take things further and overdose on pattern, from wallpapered walls to patterned floors. Do this and you've jumped rather than tiptoed into the wild side of pattern! Or you can go more subtle, it's up to you. Daring or considered, there is no wrong and no right.

Put pattern on repeat. One patterned cushion alone will seem insignificant, but when you repeat it over and over you get movement, energy and a sense of excitement. Building pattern into a room adds so much character. It gives the room clout.

It's all in the mix: graphic with organic, leopard print with florals. It's also quite interesting to mix cultures: Indian, European and American perhaps, all hanging out with each other.

Maximalism at its best has a common theme running through it, some kind of link, and by using pattern you are making your home incredibly exciting and colourful but also true to you. When you add prints and colours that you love it becomes an extension of your personality – your home will reflect that. Don't feel pressurized into buying into certain trends – just go with what makes you happy. Mixing motifs, styles and hues makes for a surprising and engaging home.

There is, of course, a fine balancing act between eclectic and messy. Considered maximalist interiors connect the dots, relating and linking motifs, scale and colour. As the eye moves around the room from one piece to the next the whole space feels balanced and when rooms feel balanced they read as beautiful!

Mixing patterns is one of those areas people tend to shy away from but it's the easiest thing you can possibly do to elevate your home. Oh and remember this: there is always room for one more pattern!

When you add prints and colours that you love it becomes an extension of your personality – your home will reflect that.

LITTLE

BLACK

BOOK

Here's my own personal directory of international secret addresses, from art to wallpaper, ceramics to furniture. It includes 'don't tell anyone' flea markets tucked away behind little back streets in Paris and hardly known addresses in Brooklyn and Byron Bay.

ABIGAIL AHERN

www.abigailahern.com
Heralded in *The New York Times* as a 'wonderland' Abigail's store houses handthrown vases, furniture, lighting, accessories, handwoven textiles, paint and her world-famous collection of faux botanicals. Recognized as one of the world's leading tastemakers, Abigail's store is rife with her unique ranges making her signature style instantly recognizable.

GENERAL

AUSTRALIA
Ici et Là
Australia
www.icietla.com.au

EUROPE
By Mölle
www.bymolle.com
Linen, throws, accessories.

Caravane
www.caravane.fr

Deyrolle
www.deyrolle.com

Maisons du Monde
www.maisonsdumonde.com

Rossana Orlandi
www.rossanaorlandi.com

La Trésorerie
www.latresorerie.fr

UK
Anglepoise
www.anglepoise.com

Nest
www.nest.co.uk

Rowen & Wren
www.rowenandwren.co.uk

UK & JAPAN
Labour and Wait
www.labourandwait.co.uk

UK & USA
West Elm
www.westelm.com

USA
ABC Carpet & Home
www.abchome.com

All Modern
www.allmodern.com

John Derian
www.johnderian.com

The Future Perfect
www.thefutureperfect.com

Homenature
www.homenature.com

Joybird
www.joybird.com

Lulu and Georgia
www.luluandgeorgia.com

Schoolhouse
www.schoolhouse.com

Super Marché Shop
www.sfgirlbybay.com/shop

Kelly Wearstler
www.kellywearstler.com

World Market
www.worldmarket.com

GLOBAL
1stdibs
www.1stdibs.com

Fatboy
www.fatboy.com

Lane Crawford
www.lanecrawford.com
Based in Hong Kong (China).

ACCESSORIES

AUSTRALIA
The Dharma Door
www.thedharmadoor.com.au
Amazing baskets, throws
and bags.

Imprint House
www.imprinthouse.net
Baskets, throws, bags
and storage.

The Society Inc
www.thesocietyinc.com.au
Hooks, handles and accessories.

EUROPE
&Tradition
www.andtradition.com
Based in Aarhus but
stocked globally.

Buly 1803
www.Buly1803.com

Frama
www.framacph.com
Based in Copenhagen but
stocked globally.

La Redoute
www.laredoute.co.uk

Le Petit Atelier e Paris
www.lepetitatelierdeparis.
bigcartel.com

Tasja P. Ceramics
www.tasjaceramics.com
Beautiful ceramics.

UK
Anthropologie
www.anthropologie.com

Cox & Cox
www.coxandcox.co.uk

Heals
www.heals.com

Nkuku
www.nkuku.com

Rose & Grey
www.roseandgrey.co.uk

USA
Bon Ton Studio
www.bonton-studio.com
Baskets, accessories and textiles.

The Citizenry
www.the-citizenry.com
Textiles, throws and accessories.

FURNITURE

AUSTRALIA
Guy Mathews
www.guymathewsindustrial.com

EUROPE
Dusty Deco
www.dustydeco.com

UK
BoConcept
www.boconcept.com

Case Furniture
www.casefurniture.com

Heals
www.heals.com

Mint
www.mintshop.co.uk
Sustainable design gallery.

MCM House
www.mcmhouse.com

George Smith
www.georgesmith.com

USA
Jonathan Adler
www.jonathanadler.com

City Foundry
www.cityfoundry.com
Upscale antiques.

McGee & Co
www.mcgeeandco.com

Kelly Wearstler
www.kellywearstler.com

LIGHTING

AUSTRALIA
Beacon Lighting
www.beaconlighting.com.au

Domayne
www.domayne.com.au

Temple & Webster
www.templeandwebster.com.au

EUROPE
Dusty Deco
www.dustydeco.com

UK
Coggles
www.coggles.com

Curiousa & Curiousa
www.curiousa.co.uk

Mint
www.mintshop.co.uk
Sustainable design gallery.

MCM House
www.mcmhouse.com

OUTDOOR FURNITURE

EUROPE
Maisons du Monde
www.maisonsdumonde.com
From hanging armchairs to
rattan rocking chairs to recycled
chic armchairs.

UK
Nest
www.nest.co.uk
From chairs, to lamps, to
outdoor stools – there's quite a
selection.

Rowen & Wren
www.rowenandwren.co.uk
Furniture, wall planters, pots
(I especially like the Harmen
Outdoor Chair!).

George Smith
www.georgesmith.com

USA
Croft House
www.crofthouse.com

West Elm
www.westelm.com
There is a much better selection
available in the USA (as opposed
to the UK), especially when it
comes to outdoor sofas.

OUTDOOR LIGHTING

UK
Anglepoise
www.anglepoise.com
Have produced lighting for
outdoors, including massive
floor lamps with marine-grade
materials as well as wall lights
with an IP65 rating to withstand
all sorts of different weather
conditions.

Curiousa & Curiousa
www.curiousa.co.uk
A great range of outdoor
lighting.

GLOBAL
Fatboy
www.fatboy.com
Floor and table lamps
specifically made for outside.

DECKING AND CABINS

Arvesund
www.arvesund.com
The shed of all sheds, Mats
Theselius designed the Hermit
Cabin with the Swedish design
firm Arvesund. It's a one-
person-only, all-season hut made
of reclaimed barn timber. Oh,
and while in the cabin you must
read this: A Place of My Own:
The Architecture of Daydreams,
Michael Pollan.

Millboard
www.millboard.co.uk
For the most incredible decking
on the planet. I'm using it
indoors as well. Their boards
are modelled on a 100-year-
old piece of oak – they aren't
actually wood though so are
indestructible.

BATHROOMS

AUSTRALIA
Bed Bath N' Table
www.bedbathntable.com.au

Design Bathware
www.designbathware.com.au

Kohler
www.kohler.com.au

Harvey Norman
www.harveynorman.com.au

EUROPE
Déco Nature
www.deco-nature.com

Muuto
www.muuto.com

Les Savons Gemme
www.savons-gemme.com

Wall and Decò
www.wallanddecò.com

Zieta
www.zieta.pl
I particularly love the Pin Wall
Hooks and Kamm Coat Rack.

UK
Bohemia
www.bohemiadesign.co.uk

Crittall
www.crittall-windows.co.uk

C.P. Hart
www.cphart.co.uk

Nest
www.nest.co.uk

MADE
www.made.com
I love their Apartment Wall

Hooks.
Majestic
www.majesticshowers.com

Mandarin Stone
www.mandarinstone.com

Marble Mosaics
www.marble-mosaics.com

Aston Matthews
www.astonmatthews.co.uk

Polyvine
www.polyvine.com

Retrouvius
www.retrouvius.com

Victorian Plumbing
www.victorianplumbing.co.uk

The Water Monopoly
www.thewatermonopoly.com

Wickes
www.wickes.co.uk

USA
Bed Bath & Beyond
www.bedbathandbeyond.com

Joss & Main
www.jossandmain.com

Restoration Hardware
www.restorationhardware.com

Waterworks
www.waterworks.com

FLOORING

AUSTRALIA
Beaumont Tiles
www.connollys.com.au

National Tiles
www.nationaltiles.com.au

Connollys Timber Flooring
www.connollys.com.au

EUROPE
Ciment Flooring
www.cimentfactory.com

Casalgrande Padana
www.casalgrandepadana.com

Kasthall
www.kasthall.com

UK
Ecora
www.ecora.co.uk

Emily's House
www.emilyshouselondon.com

Christopher Farr
www.christopherfarr.com

Flooring Centre
www.flooringsuppliescentre.
co.uk

Larusi
www.larusi.com

Mandarin Stone
www.mandarinstone.com

Millboard
www.millboard.co.uk

The New & Reclaimed
Flooring Co.
www.reclaimedflooringco.com

Puur
www.puurfloors.com

Senso
www.sensofloors.co.uk

Solid Floor
www.solidfloor.co.uk

Victorian Woodworks
www.woodworksbytedtodd.com

USA
Amtico
www.amtico.com

Mohawk Flooring
www.mohawkflooring.com

Shaw Floors
www.shawfloors.com

WALLS

AUSTRALIA
Artisan Paint
www.artisanpaintcompany.com.
au

Bauwerk Colour
www.bauwerk.com.au

Instyle
www.instyle.com.au

EUROPE

Emery & Cie
www.emeryetcie.com

Made a Mano
www.madeamano.com

MOROCCO
Popham Design
www.pophamdesign.com

UK
Barracuda
www.barracuda-distribution.
co.uk

Bert & May
www.bertandmay.com

The Colour Flooring Company
www.colourflooring.co.uk

Dreamwall
www.dreamwall.co.uk

Jelinek Cork Group
www.corkstore.co.uk
www.jelinek.com

Milagros
www.milagros.co.uk

Sinclair Till
www.sinclairtill.co.uk

Wallpaper UK
www.wallpaper-uk.com

USA
Benjamin Moore
www.benjaminmoore.com/en-us

Decorators Best
www.decoratorsbest.com

Home Depot
www.homedepot.com

Phillip Jeffries
www.phillipjeffries.com

Wayfair.com
www.wayfair.com

BRICK WALLS

AUSTRALIA
Brickworks
www.brickworks.com.au

Creative Bricks
www.creativebricks.com.au

Eco Outdoor
www.ecooutdoor.com.au

UK
Ashwell Timber
www.ashwelltimber.com

Brick Slips
www.brickslips.net

Lassco
www.lassco.co.uk

Reclaimed Brick-Tile
www.reclaimedbrick-tile.com

Windsor Reclamation
www.reclaimed-brick.co.uk

USA
Gavin Historical Bricks
www.historicalbricks.com

Stikwood
www.stikwood.com

WALLPAPER

EUROPE
Arte
www.arte-international.com

Wall & Decò
www.wallanddeco.com

UK
Cole & Son
www.cole-and-son.com

de Gournay
www.degournay.com

Graham & Brown
www.grahambrown.com

House of Hackney
www.houseofhackney.com
Showrooms in London and
New York.

Tracy Kendall
www.tracykendall.com

Rebel Walls
www.rebelwalls.co.uk

USA
Phillip Jeffries
www.phillipjeffries.com

NLXL
www.nlxl.com

ART AND DECOR

AUSTRALIA
Bromley & Co.
www.bromleyandco.com

Edo Arts
www.edoarts.com.au

JAI VASICEK GALLERY
www.jaivasicek.com

EUROPE
Absolut Art
www.absolutart.com

L'Objet Qui Parle
www.lobjetquiparle.fr

UK
Artfinder
www.artfinder.com

New Blood Art
www.newbloodart.com

Saatchi Art
www.saatchiart.com

USA
20 x 200
www.20x200.com

Aha
www.ahalife.com

ArtStar
www.artstar.com

Exhibition A
www.exhibitiona.com

Juniper Print Ship
www.juniperprintshop.com

Lumas
www.lumas.com

Minted
www.minted.com

Society 6
www.society6.com

Tappan
www.tappancollective.com

Tiny Showcase
www.tinyshowcase.com

World Market
www.worldmarket.com

GLOBAL
Affordable Art Fair
www.affordableartfair.com

Etsy
www.etsy.com

Unsplash
www.unsplash.com

Zatista
www.zatista.com

BEDDING

EUROPE
Caravane
www.caravane.fr

Merci
www.merci-merci.com

Society Limonta
www.societylimonta.com

UK
Gingerlily
www.gingerlily.co.uk

MCM House
www.mcmhouse.com

SCENT

CANADA, USA & EUROPE
Urban Outfitters
www.urbanoutfitters.com

UK
Neom
www.neomorganics.com

USA
Saje
www.saje.com

USA & EUROPE
Anthropologie
www.anthropologie.com
For the Ekobo Essential Oil
Diffuser and Vitruvi Black
Stone Oil Diffuser.

GLOBAL
Aesop
www.aesop.com

LeLabo
www.lelabofragrances.com
For the Santal 26 Home
Diffuser.

Muji
www.muji.com

RUGS

UK
Larusi
www.larusi.com

Maroc Tribal
www.maroctribal.com
Modern Rugs
www.modern-rugs.co.uk

Affordable rugs.
Roger Oates Design
ww.rogeroates.com

USA & EUROPE
Anthropologie
www.anthropologie.com

USA
ABC Carpet & Home
www.abchome.com

Jayson Home
www.jaysonhome.com

Joss & Main
www.jossandmain.com

Lulu and Georgia
www.luluandgeorgia.com

One Kings Lane
www.onekingslane.com

Overstock
www.overstock.com

Parachute
www.parachutehome.com

World Market
www.worldmarket.com

ISRAEL
Beija Flor
www.beijaflorworld.com

UPHOLSTERY

AUSTRALIA
Ici et Là
www.icietla.com.au

UK
House of Hackney
www.houseofhackney.
comShowrooms in London and
New York.

ANTIQUES AND VINTAGE

EUROPE
Marché aux Puces
www.marcheauxpuces-
saintouen.com
This market is huge – you can
find things costing from a
couple of euros, to zillions.

Porte de Vanves, Paris
My favourite flea, hardly
any tourists and some
incredible stuff.

UK
Alfie's Antique Market
www.alfiesantiques.com
This famous London indoor
market houses a beautiful
selection of vintage pieces.
It's not cheap but you'll
probably find things you
won't see elsewhere.

The International Antiques and
Collectors Fairs
www.iacf.co.uk
Forty antiques fairs in seven
locations across the year,
throughout the year. From
antiques and collectables to
vintage clothing.

USA
Big Daddy's Antiques
www.bdantiques.com
Antiques and reproductions
from Europe, Asia and North
America.

INTERIOR DESIGN APPS

RoomScan Pro
It draws floor plans by itself –
you simply hold your phone up
to the wall and watch it scan the
circumference of the room.

Homestyler
www.homestyler.com
This is another app that has a
ton of useful features, including
the ability to place 3D models of
real furniture in your own room.

Acknowledgements

My name might be on the cover of this tome, but I am just a very small part of it and it's my team that I owe the hugest thanks to – Imran Jadwet, Ed Patten, Sheila Anderson, Maya Plescher, Hollie Seatherton and Russ Lewis. Your perfectionism and tremendous hard work mean the world.

Special thanks, as always, to Gem (biz partner and sister), we've worked side by side for over 15 years now and none of this would be possible without you. Thank you.

Thanks also to the team at Pavilion, in particular Helen Lewis, who gave me this incredible opportunity for a fourth book!

To my family and my incredible parents, who I love so much. To Lils, Thea, Jude, Hols and Lee – I love you guys, and of course Gem and Russ, family and biz partners who have helped shape and create the most fabulous business.

The hugest thank-you to you the readers and my fabulous community of supporters. You are such an incredibly supportive, welcoming and amazing bunch of people. Thank you so very much.

Thank you to the Urban Cowboy hotels (a beautiful collection of boutique hotels in Nashville, TN and the Catskill Mountains). All photographs of the hotels taken by Ben Fitchett.

Thank you also to Sophie Ashby for sharing such fabulous pictures of her home; and to Alex Bagner, writer, editor and co-owner of the boutique hotel, bar and restaurant, The Rose, Deal for opening up her beautiful house. Thank you also to Jelle Van de Schoor and Theo-Bert Pot for letting us photograph their incredibly beautiful Hague apartment and providing us with such delicious baked goods.

To Graham Atkins Hughes for always taking so many beautiful images and being my best bud.

And also to Caitlin Mills and Lucy Feagins at The Design Files, Gaelle le Boulicaut, Kara Rosulund and the Sisters Agency.

Photography acknowledgements

Pages 7, 8, 21, 24, 34, 42, 48–49, 53, 57, 62–63, 86, 87, 93, 97, 101, 114–115, 125, 129, 130, 136–137, 139, 149, 153, 154, 159, 162, 163, 165, 166–167, 169, 172–173, 174, 177, 178, 180, 181, 186, 187, 194, 199, 205, 215, 217, 218, 222, 226–227, 243, 254: photography by Graham Atkins-Hughes

Pages 14, 26, 27, 32, 61, 150-151, 192, 209, 221, 230: photography by Birgitta Wolfgang Bjornvad/The Sisters Agency

Pages 22-23, 47, 50, 126-127, 146-147, 182-183, 231, 234-235: design by Lyon Porter, photography by Ben Fitchett for the Urban Cowboy Hotels

Pages 4, 43, 64–65, 70, 95, 170: Apartment designed by Sophie Ashby, founder of Studio Ashby; Photography by Alexander James, styling by Olivia Gregory

Pages 11, 16, 28, 41, 52, 99, 110, 121, 135, 145, 252–253: Maryam Mahdavi's location, photography by Gaelle le Boulicaut; 19, 31, 39, 45, 76, 105, 232, 241: Laurence Leenaert's location, photography by Gaelle le Boulicaut; 74, 96, 124, 138, 160-161, 195, 229 Sandra Benhamou's location, photography by Gaelle le Boulicaut

Pages 2, 73, 132-133, 175, 206-207: the home of Alex McCabe, photography by Caitlin Mills / The Design Files; 30, 75, 90-91, 185, 188–189, 210, 224-225, 249: the home of Mardi Ola, photography by Caitlin Mills / The Design Files; 13, 78–79, 80-81, 82, 102-103, 118, 191, 239: the home of Rachel Castle, photography by Caitlin Mills / The Design Files; 15, 89, 122–123, 196–197: the home of Natalie Walton, photography by Caitlin Mills / The Design Files

Pages 37, 54-55, 58, 59, 66, 69, 85, 92, 106, 113, 117, 140, 143, 144, 157, 200. 201 202, 211, 213, 236: photography by Kara Rosenlund

First published in the United Kingdom in 2020 by Pavilion
43 Great Ormond Street
London
WC1N 3HZ

Copyright © Pavilion Books Company Ltd 2020
Text copyright © Abigail Ahern 2020

ISBN 978-1-91164-111-7

A CIP catalogue record for this book is available from the British Library.

10 9 8 7 6 5 4 3 2 1

Reproduction by Rival London Ltd
Printed and bound by 1010 Printing
International Ltd
www.pavilionbooks.com

Publisher: Helen Lewis
Design: Laura Russell and Nikki Ellis
Project editors: Lucy Smith and Sophie Allen
Copy editor: Amy Christian
Production Manager: Phil Brown

FSC
www.fsc.org
MIX
Paper from responsible sources
FSC® C016973